PRAISE FOR *MAKE SOMEONE'S DAY*

"Just by reading the title I was inspired to *Make Someone's Day* a few times that same day. But when you dig deeper, this book uncovers many ways to do it, depending on who you are interacting with and for which occasion. *Make Someone's Day* unleashes positive energy, and that is great per se; however, as a CEO I know how instrumental it is to apply it to thrive as a company and as an organization"

—**Fabrizio Parini, CEO, Lindt & Sprüngli SpA Italy (Lindt Chocolate)**

"At a time when leaders are bemoaning the 'soft skills gap' that plagues many workplaces, Howard offers an answer. *Make Someone's Day* provides a simple road map that if embraced and followed, could transform workplaces."

—**Tony Bingham, president and CEO, Association for Talent Development (ATD)**

"The magic of *Make Someone's* Day is that it's so easy to use and it works! A culture where people are happy and engaged is powerful, rewarding, and makes sense. I love the idea and the impact it has. Let's all step up and do this."

—**Garry Ridge, chairman and CEO, WD-40 Company**

"I'm thrilled to see *Make Someone's Day* come to fruition after collaborating with Howard Prager for the past year on my organization's new leadership program. Howard embodies his philosophy in each interaction, and it has been an honor to learn the lessons he shares in his book directly through our work together. His approach aligns with our organization's mission and my personal mission to make the workplace better for all. If all CEOs apply these concepts, we can build a more productive, inspiring, and inclusive business world."

—**Valentina T. Parissi, president and CEO, Great Books Foundation**

"*Make Someone's Day* is desperately needed in a world that is often too busy to do what matters most. Howard H. Prager brings both science and heart to some of the biggest leadership challenges—inspiration, motivation, and engagement.

These should be key focus areas for every organization and leader, especially at this critical time of recovery in the world."

—Jennifer McCollum, CEO, Linkage, Inc.

"With a simple yet powerful message, Howard H. Prager shows just how important it is to take care of one another. This practical guide is the key to so much of what's essential to work today—positive and inspiring employee experience, better business results, and an inspired and engaged workforce."

—Mike Prokopeak, editor in chief at *Reworked,* host of *Get Reworked* podcast, and former editor in chief at *Chief Learning Officer* magazine

"Every leader wants to create healthy, thriving organizations where employees are committed to success—and *Make Someone's Day* shows us a simple and powerful way to do it. If you want to benefit your employees, your company, and yourself at the same time, read this book now!"

—Dorie Clark, author of *Reinventing You,* and executive education faculty, Duke University Fuqua School of Business

"With inspiring stories and a clear, actionable guide, Howard Prager does a masterful job of helping us show up, be there, and make someone's day better, no matter where we are or what we are doing. *Make Someone's Day* will inspire you to bring positivity and gratitude wherever you go. *Make Someone's Day* is a timeless read for anyone striving to be a thoughtful leader and make long-lasting, meaningful impacts through small yet powerful daily actions."

—Erica Dhawan, author of *Digital Body Language*

"This book is brimming with practical examples of ways to make someone's day at work with easy-to-implement tools. This book should be in every manager's toolkit!"

—Dr. Tasha Eurich, organizational psychologist, and *New York Times* bestselling author of *Insight* and *Bankable Leadership*

"Having measured the impact of thousands of leaders and managers on the people around them, I can assure you that your words and actions have a profound effect on the behavior and performance of your direct reports, peers, and even your superiors. Do them all a favor and read Howard H. Prager's book to get some great ideas for making that impact as positive, productive, and cheerful as possible."

—Robert A. Cooke, PhD, CEO, Human Synergistics International, and author of *Leadership/Impact* and the *Organizational Culture Inventory*

"Just as sprinkles make a cupcake special, this delightful book is the recipe for adding joy to the lives of others. I could not put it down and learned so much about how to magically and memorably *Make Someone's Day*."

—Chip R. Bell, author of *Inside Your Customer's Imagination*

"Make Someone's Day provides a powerful reminder of the amazing impact each of us can have on the lives of other people. Howard's book includes a practical guide that helps you get started asap."

—Harry M. Jansen Kraemer, Jr., clinical professor of leadership, Northwestern University Kellogg School of Management, former chairman and CEO, Baxter International

"This book should have been titled *Make My Day*. That's how you will feel after following Howard Prager's eminently practical advice in *Make Someone's Day*. Sunny and optimistic, reading his book certainly made mine."

—Whitney Johnson, bestselling author of *Disrupt Yourself* and *Build an A Team*

"The power of being appreciated goes beyond being thanked. It's being *seen*. This short book, full of stories and ideas, can help you give the gift of humanity."

—Michael Bungay Stanier, bestselling author of *The Coaching Habit*

"In *Make Someone's Day*, Howard Prager reminds us that a core human need is to feel connected, be uplifted, and be inspired to take on the world's challenges. He deftly combines compelling stories with pragmatic steps that you can take to make a difference at work, at home, and in your life."

—Charlene Li, founder of Altimeter and *NYTimes* bestselling author of *The Disruption Mindset*

"This gentle, uplifting book reminds us of our human power to touch and shape the lives of others so easily with a glittering instant of kindness. Maybe a single sentence—the easy act of noticing, appreciating, putting our words around something special in the person before us and giving it to them—words likely to be forgotten by the giver, but maybe written forever on the walls of the receiver's heart. Simply seizing a tiny moment, capturing the glory of an individual, and sharing it with them. Others have done this for me and you alike, giving us words they never realized we'd treasure for years. I love this book."

—Price Pritchett, PhD, CEO, Pritchett, LP

"*Make Someone's Day* shifts our leadership approach from transactional to relational. We see the impact that helping others can have; it acts as a force multiplier that pays off well beyond just motivating people and helping them get things done. It engenders loyalty, builds trust, and puts humanity back into the workplace, which is something many organizations urgently need.

"You know that feeling when someone does something helpful for you? You're not only thankful, you're more loyal to them, you feel valued, and you want to pass it on. As Prager points out, being kind and supportive in the workplace isn't just a good thing to do; it's a contagious force that drives people to collaborate, better understand each other, and get more valuable things done.

"Humanity in the workplace is often talked about but rarely truly valued; leaders are focused on the bottom line. But as employees reevaluate what work means to them in a post-COVID world, they realize that truly supportive work environments don't just matter, they are in fact essential. Leaders that retool their approach to put their time into supporting people vs. processes and procedures will rise above the rest."

—Lisa Bodell, futurist and CEO, FutureThink

"*Make Someone's Day* definitely made mine. Prager offers an in-depth look at how we can use kindness to improve our life and the lives of those around us. The book is well researched and filled with practical tips. Should be on everyone's to-read list."

—Eva Ritvo, MD, author and founder, Bekindr

"Great positive advice from one of the most uplifting individuals we know. Full of tips, techniques, tools, and proven applications, this book makes it easy for you to bring out the best in people with a very positive approach. This book is helpful for your work situations and family and community relationships as well. It's a post-pandemic must-read."

—**Patti P. Phillips, PhD, CEO, and Jack J. Phillips, PhD, chairman of ROI Institute; authors of over 100 books**

"*Make Someone's Day* brings kindness and caring to the workplace while building leadership and manager awareness and skills. This is a must-have skill for today's leaders!"

—**Chester Elton, the Apostle of Appreciation, bestselling author of *The Carrot Principle, Leading with Gratitude,* and *Anxiety at Work***

"*Make Someone's* Day brings kindness and caring to the workplace while providing a powerful way to hone our leadership skills. After all, leaders can't succeed unless they can motivate people, making them feel included, valued, and seen. Our contentious world can benefit enormously if we can all commit to making someone's day."

—**Sally Helgesen, author of *How Women Rise, The Female Advantage,* and *The Web of Inclusion***

"This is the ideal book for our times—an instructive and inspirational guide to kindness and generosity in a wide variety of situations. Howard Prager's book will make your day!"

—**Lindsey Pollak, *New York Times* bestselling author of *Recalculating: Navigate Your Career through the Changing World of Work* and *The Remix: How to Lead and Succeed in the Multigenerational Workplace***

"Filled with stories, tips, and techniques about how we can make a difference in other people's lives, *Make Someone's* Day is a joy to read and an inspiration to be a better person."

—**Dave Vance, president and founder, Center for Talent Reporting**

"Howard Prager has a beautiful, simple, and world-changing idea: make it a habit to make someone's day. In *Make Someone's Day* he shows how simple,quick, inexpensive, and powerful acts as simple as providing a sincere compliment can be. If you want to be a more effective boss, spouse, friend, and leader, read and practice *Make Someone's Day*."

—**Roy V.H. Pollock, DVM, PhD, chief learning officer, The 6Ds Company,** co-author of *The Six Disciplines of Breakthrough Learning*

"In today's stressful, emotional, and constantly changing world, we all need more opportunities to smile and help others smile! Howard Prager's book, *Make Someone's Day*, is a timely reminder and resource to help us make our day by making someone else's day! This is a book you DO, not just a book you read. Go ahead and make your day. Read it and then *do* it!"

—**Tom Darrow, founder and principal, Talent Connections, LLC and Career Spa, LLC**

"*Make Someone's Day* provides a three-for-one. It benefits the person you're doing it for, the leader who does it, and the organization. Howard H. Prager has found a brilliant way to create healthier organizations and employees who are more committed to success. Wouldn't it be wonderful if everyone lived by these principles?"

—**Dr. Bev Kaye, co-author of *Love 'Em or Lose 'Em, Help Them Grow or Watch Them Go*, and *Up Is Not the Only Way*, speaker, thought leader**

"*Make Someone's Day* is a hands-on look at kindness in the workplace. Howard H. Prager shows through stories and examples how what we do for others can make a positive difference in our workplaces. *Make Someone's Day* provides practical tips and ideas for all of us on how to make our workplaces more desirable, more engaging, and more productive. The rewards are ample when we invest in making someone's day."

—**John Baldoni, executive coach and author of fifteen books, including *Grace Notes: Leading in an Upside Down World***

"Times of disruption challenge our nervous system and can create reactive behaviors that shut down creativity, curiosity, and collaboration just when we need it most. *Make Someone's Day* is the antidote to this reactive behavior. It teaches leaders and all of us to help others feel valued and appreciated, which in turn helps us all to be more engaged and change-agile. This is a practical book that is much needed for our times."

—Henna Inam, CEO, Transformational Leadership Inc,
author of *Wired for Disruption*

"What an eye-opener! Howard has masterfully outlined the simple things we all can do or say every day to create a butterfly effect that can have a far-reaching impact in creating a world of civility and humanity. These precious moments unleash oxytocin that provide lasting effects on our energy, spirit, attitude, and motivation. After reading *Make Someone's Day*, you will start to notice the many spontaneous opportunities to make a difference in the lives of everyone around you."

—Rita Bailey, owner, Up To Something, LLC

"*Make Someone's Day* is a joy to read and a resource that I will return to time and time again. The best leaders in our lives, at home, and at work, are the ones who connect with us on a personal level, help us to be successful, and make our day. It's all about how they make us feel. Howard Prager shares hundreds of examples of how we can all *Make Someone's Day*. It's the recipe book for connection with a whole serving of special sauce for appreciation that will inspire everyone."

—Morag Barrett, author of *Cultivate: The Power of Winning Relationships*
and *The Future-Proof Workplace*, keynote speaker, and global leadership
development expert

"It was Voltaire that first observed in the eighteenth century that 'common sense is not so common.' Such is the case with the delightfully simple idea of 'making someone's day.' We all know the special feeling that comes when someone does this for us and how it puts us in a good mood for the rest of the day, if not longer. But how many of us take the time to 'make someone's day' for others? With Howard Prager's new book, *Make Someone's Day*, doing so just got a little easier. It offers a plethora of strategies, techniques, and examples to help managers and employees alike apply this deceptively simple, yet powerful principle!"

—Dr. Bob Nelson, bestselling author of *1001 Ways to Reward Employees* and
Work Made Fun Gets Done! Easy Ways to Boost Energy, Morale, and Results

"What's not to love? Howard makes it easy for you to be generous in acknowledging and appreciating others—making a difference in someone's life—and to be a hero for it."

—Molly Tschang, creator of *Say It Skillfully*® video series and radio show

"Get ready to get inspired! This book made my day and will make my entire life better. The info on neuroscience is cutting edge and will help people train brains to be more productive."

—Gerald "Solutionman" Haman

"Howard Prager taps into the fundamental kindness our world needs now more than ever. If we all apply just one of the numerous suggestions, our world will be a better place."

—Eddie Turner, host of *Keep Leading!*® Podcast

"This book is a must-read for any mission-based entrepreneur, executive, or expert."

—Adam Torres, co-founder, Mission Matters

"I just got finished reading *Make Someone's Day: Becoming a Memorable Leader in Work and Life* by Howard Prager and all I can do is smile. As a leader, one of my most important roles is to make sure people know I value their work. Howard's book gives me so many meaningful ways I can do that with my team as a leader and with friends, family, and others in my life. This book is gold, and every leader should take the time to read it."

—Rhett Power, co-founder of Courageous Leadership

*Make Someone's Day: Becoming a Memorable
Leader in Work and Life*

by Howard H. Prager

© Copyright 2021 Howard H. Prager

ISBN 978-1-64663-441-5

Published by

◣köehlerbooks™

3705 Shore Drive
Virginia Beach, VA 23455
800-435-4811
www.koehlerbooks.com

Make Someone's Day

"Just by reading the title I was inspired to make someone's day a few times that same day."

—FABRIZIO PARINI,
CEO Lindt Chocolate
Italy

Becoming a
Memorable Leader
in Work and Life

HOWARD H. PRAGER

FOREWORD BY MARSHALL GOLDSMITH

NY Times Bestselling Author of Triggers: Creating Behavior that Lasts—
Becoming the Person You Want to Be, and Renowned Professor and Coach

VIRGINIA BEACH
CAPE CHARLES

FOREWORD

By Marshall Goldsmith

AS AN EXECUTIVE COACH for over forty years, one of the pillars of leadership I teach to my executives is humility. Practicing servant leadership can be difficult for many leaders, but it has a powerful impact on the trust and sincerity you present for your organization. One of the best examples of servant leadership I've experienced is Frances Hesselbein, who was CEO of the Girl Scouts of the USA for nearly fifteen years. Some years ago, I was asked to do a workshop for them over the weekend at the end of a long business trip. I had talked with Frances and was impressed with how she was turning around this storied organization. I got to their headquarters in New York the night before to meet with Frances and confirm our plans. She asked if there was anything I needed. I told her I'd been on the road for a while and could use some of my clothes washed. She said to leave it to her and that it was no problem. I assumed she'd have an assistant take it to a laundry facility during my presentation and have it back to me after the workshop. The next morning, I was sitting in the main lobby with the top Girl Scout executives and leaders from around the country that had come for the session. From around the corner, Frances entered the lobby carrying, much to my dismay, my pile of dirty laundry in her arms. She didn't give it to an assistant; she didn't send it out; she picked it up and was going to wash it herself. The CEO of the Girl Scouts was showing servant leadership to her executives in a big way through this small act. Frances became one of my favorite people, a mentor and a lifelong friend after that. She absolutely made my day with her actions. I believe Frances is one of the greatest leaders of all time for her stalwart and servant-centered leadership.

My good friend Howard Prager has come up with this beautiful idea called Make Someone's Day, and it's similar to the feeling I had when Frances did my laundry. His idea is that when we do something for others that's so impactful for them that they say, "You made my day," it's a powerful win-win concept. You have strongly impacted the other person, and in response, your emotions reflect the gratitude of the person whose day you made. Simple. Yet, for some reason, people don't do this very often. There's an issue of trust, suspicion, and a nagging thought of, "What's the catch?"

My career in coaching has been focused on making good leaders even better. How many of you think that the best way to be a boss is to control and manage your employees tightly to ensure no mistakes ever get made? Bzzzz. Not quite. Our job as leaders is to help people be their best selves, do their best work, and even be inspired in the process. That's what Make Someone's Day is all about. If we want a win-win for our employees and our jobs, why not inspire them first? Do their "laundry" or whatever they may need at that time! That way, they're more motivated to do a great job. What's more, you get a bonus! When they say, "You made my day," you get a positive jolt of energy back in return.

There are a few keys that Howard explains in the book. He describes the simple process he created to make someone's day, which he calls The VIP Model. Who doesn't want to feel like a VIP? He describes the science behind how it works and shares many stories and examples shared throughout the book so you can visualize how you can make someone's day. Howard poses some questions and brief application activities at the end of each chapter so you can put these skills into practice right away.

This is a valuable concept and can be used by bosses, leaders, and truly everyone. We can all take the opportunity to make someone's day, every day. It's easy, it's painless, it's free, and there's a good chance you will get a return. Sounds like a no brainer to me!

Life is good.
Marshall Goldsmith

DEDICATION

· ·

This book is dedicated to my parents, Sally and Arnold Prager, and my grandmother, Jennie Davis. It's through them that I learned the value of making someone's day. I will be forever grateful.

INTRODUCTION

· ·

"No act of kindness, no matter how small, is ever wasted." —Aesop

IT WAS MY TENTH birthday, and my family wanted to surprise me with an afternoon outing. The only problem was that I had a paper route, the weekend paper came out late Saturday morning, and I had to deliver them by one p.m. If we were going to my surprise, they had to be done by twelve thirty or sooner. How was I going to deliver the papers and get to the surprise activity? Typically, the papers were dropped off at my house and I had to rubber band them together before I delivered them throughout the neighborhood. My dad had a different idea. He called the South Evanston News Agency and found out that their office had a machine that automatically tied newspapers with string. He got permission for us to pick up the papers there and use the machine to rapidly tie the papers. He then drove me on my paper route. That way I could meet my responsibilities and enjoy the birthday surprise (an outing at Wrigley Field to see the Chicago Cubs baseball game that afternoon). That's a great example of one of the ways my dad made my day at my first job, ensuring I met my obligations *and* had a good birthday. Has your parent, uncle, aunt, or friend ever come to your rescue in one of your jobs? Have you ever gotten a little help at work when you needed it that made your day?

Michelle knew her employee's son loved soccer, so when she was on vacation in Argentina, she picked up a soccer (football) jersey. Not just any jersey but a Lionel Messi jersey, one of the greatest Argentinian players. When she got back from her trip, she gave it to her employee, who burst into tears. Why? "She was on vacation thousands of miles from home, and she thought about me, my son, and what he might like. What message did that send? That she cared about what was most important to me." Michelle indeed made her employee's day. How productive and committed will that employee be? Acts of kindness and caring are powerful because they connect us at a human level and demonstrate that your employees are on your mind, that you care about them and know what's important to them, even when away from the office.

After consulting with them for several months, the Lake Forest Graduate School of Management invited me to join their staff and lead executive education. I happily accepted. On my first week there, they asked if I would join a faculty member to go to Harvard Business School and take a workshop to learn how to teach the case study method, then teach the graduate school faculty when we returned. It made my day that they asked me, and I treasure the weekend I spent in Cambridge learning this skill I had experienced as a graduate business school student myself. Have you been asked to take a course that you realized was something you wanted to do? Isn't it great when that works out, sometimes by chance and sometimes because you have made your interests and preferences known?

Neville shares a customer service experience that's sadly all too rare—someone truly taking the time to listen and resolve our issues. "Sometimes you are lucky and just speak to someone who really cares. I had to call a financial services center last week. The company concerned had made life difficult with their online service, phrasing things in a language I didn't immediately understand. The person who answered the call recognized my stress levels and quickly and skillfully eased them by taking responsibility, managing the call, and coordinating with other departments. I have told over twenty-five people about this fabulous customer service. This person was basically doing their job, but really well." This should be the rule, not the exception in customer service, because when they happen, they certainly stand out and make our day.

I often bike on local errands. When I got home from one of these rides, I couldn't find my wallet. Where had I left it? Had it fallen out while biking? I didn't think so. In a bit of panic for all the IDs and credit cards I'd need to replace, I drove back to the store, following the route I took, scanning the ground intensely in case I dropped the wallet while biking. I got to the store and retraced my steps then asked the manager if a wallet had been turned in. Nothing. Dejected, I drove home thinking about which credit card to call first. As I was starting to look up my credit card numbers, there was a knock at the door. Someone saw my wallet outside the store, picked it up, found my address on my driver's license, and drove over to return it! I felt so relieved and grateful. Have you ever lost something that someone found and returned? It's such a good feeling to have that end well, and it does make your day.

Irene, the board president of an association I worked for, told me that my ears should have been burning—people were saying great things about my work. I had been having my doubts about how well I was doing in this new job, and that unsolicited comment absolutely made my day. I don't know if she realized my concerns, but she cleared them up nicely with that remark. Making someone's day can be the smallest of comments, most innocent of acts, and not cost a cent. It just needs to happen.

I've often written journal articles throughout my career for managers, leaders, HR, and talent development professionals. Leadership development is one of the topics I frequently write about. I have been deeply concerned about the lack of effectiveness of leadership development and proposed an article to *Talent Development Journal* titled "Fixing the Crisis in Leadership Development," which they accepted. I worked diligently on the article, giving them my very best thinking. A few months later, I got several advance copies in the mail. I opened the package and let out a yell. My wife wondered what had happened. My article had been chosen as the cover article for that issue! Never did I expect this would happen. That truly made my day.

As a trainer at Disney, Lenn and many others worked long hours over several months to prepare Animal Kingdom to open at Walt Disney World. Afterward, the team members were all rewarded with a sneak preview of the park before it opened to the public, several guest passes, and a special memento as part of the opening team. These perks can motivate us to go above and beyond in our jobs. It doesn't take much, just appreciation for going above and beyond to meet a goal. It's often this small recognition and acknowledgement that encourages us to continue working so hard to accomplish major projects. Over twenty years later, Lenn fondly remembers that. These memories when someone makes your day can last a lifetime.

An unexpected compliment came to me when I was playing tuba at Temple. As a tuba player, I typically play the bass line. Since we had a bass player that night, I played a melodic counterpoint to the music, filling in the gaps and supporting the melody as I've heard our reed player and violist do so well. I wasn't sure how I was fitting into this more unusual role for a tuba. At the end of the evening, the choir director came over and said what a difference I made in the band! Another made-my-day moment, totally unexpected, and with the added credibility from someone who is a trained musician. Thanks, Gail!

Do you begin to see a pattern here? Make Someone's Day moments are often spontaneous, unsolicited comments or actions that make your spirit soar. They can confirm you've made the right decision and taken the right action. They can lift you up when you're feeling uncertain. They can remove doubt, return wallets, and take you to places and to people you'd never otherwise get to or meet. That's why Make Someone's Day moments are so powerful. They come unexpectedly and often at the perfect time when they're most needed. Timing is critical. If these comments were said another time, it may have been nice to hear but not have made someone's day. If I just got my paper route done faster that June day when I was turning ten, it would have been nice but wouldn't have meant as much if my dad didn't want to show me that I could meet my obligations and enjoy a birthday surprise. Irene and Gail, through their unsolicited comments, made me feel better as an employee and musician. I prominently display the Harvard Business School Press book *Teaching Using the Case Study Method* on my bookshelf, as well as my cover of the *TD Journal*. All proud reminders of how people have made my day and the memorable moments they create.

Wharton Professor Adam Grant, in his book *Give and Take*, talks about givers, people who give to others without expectations, much like people who make someone's day. One of the key insights he found is that "successful givers enjoy professional relationships that last longer and reap more long-term benefits than relationships with takers or matchers."

What did someone do for you that really brightened up your day and made a difference for you? When did this happen and why? This could be intentional or not, planned or unplanned. Think back to a time from work or growing up when a comment from a boss, colleague, instructor, or friend came when you most needed it. They may have complimented you, offered advice, shared a snack, recommended a course, encouraged you to pursue ways to grow, or just been there to support you when you most needed it. I was truly blessed with a few good bosses and especially have found great mentors throughout my career from my profession along with some terrific colleagues who became lifetime friends. Growing up, I was fortunate to have wonderful parents, caring teachers, an excellent Scoutmaster, and band directors. They all encouraged me throughout life and often made my day, giving me needed confidence to persevere. Take a moment right now and identify who played a big role in your life at work or growing up. These are memorable leaders creating memorable moments. What actions did they do, say, or show to support and encourage you? Has that stayed with you? That's remarkable, isn't it?

That's what this book is about, learning the simple VIP Model I share in chapter two and reading about some of the many ways you can make someone's day and be a better leader, manager, teammate, friend, colleague, or family member committed to creating memorable moments. I believe "you made my day" can be the strongest and best compliment we can get. Because whatever you did was particularly needed, welcomed, and appreciated at that time. People don't say that randomly. Think about it—when did someone last say to you, "You made my day," or you saw a smile or reaction that indicated the same sort of thing? Did you ask yourself, "What did I do?" Did you think about how it made you feel when you heard those words? It's a goosebumps moment. Your body lights up, and whatever type of day you're having becomes so much better, let alone the person who was impacted in such a significant way that urged them to say, "You made my day."

HOW IT ALL STARTED

The first time I realized the powerful impact of Make Someone's Day was at the train station with other early morning commuters waiting for our train downtown. A young woman with a clipboard came up asking me to sign her petition to put someone on the ballot for election. In Illinois, in order to be on an election ballot, you have to gain a certain number of signatures on a petition first. I asked who it was for, and when I learned, I said I'd heard of him and would happily sign. I saw that I was the first person to sign her petition. As I handed her back the clipboard, she looked up at me and exclaimed, "You made my day!" Those words took me by surprise. I don't know how many people she had asked before me. Had she been turned down or ignored? Was this the first time she was gathering signatures on a petition? All it took from me was the simple act of signing my name on the petition and that made her day. And in turn, it made me feel great when she said that. My commute, the morning, even the day was totally different. I had been feeling good, but this brought it to a higher level. And it wasn't about what I did, it was *remembering what she said*: "You made my day." Those words made my day, too, through what I call the boomerang effect, which I'll explain more in chapter three.

That whole train ride downtown, I could think of nothing else. My mood shifted from ordinary to extraordinary. Work was fantastic. I couldn't imagine how such a little action could have that type of impact. It raised my awareness and got me thinking about how important it is in all of our lives, especially in these crazy and challenging times when everyone is so focused on themselves and bracing for what life is throwing us next. The simple act of making someone's day needs to be shared and brought to a more conscious—and conscientious—level. If we can all strive to make someone's day every day, what a powerful impact it can leave on us, on others around us, on our companies, on our community, and even on the world.

WHO THIS BOOK IS FOR

If you're a leader or manager, this book will help you be a great one by using Make Someone's Day to inspire your staff and colleagues. Think of the stronger performance, productivity, and commitment people will have if you do this on a regular basis.

If you're a colleague, why not bring joy to others, since we're all in this together?

If you're a friend or just someone who cares about others, what better way to excite them than by making someone's day? As you'll see in the first few chapters, it can be very simple to do, and in later chapters, you'll read about examples of using Make Someone's Day in various parts of your work and life, even making someone's day online while creating lasting impact in the process.

WHAT YOU WILL LEARN

This book will teach you ways to make someone's day, small and large, planned and unplanned, in person and online. You'll learn many actions that every leader, manager, and person can do to make someone's day. You'll become more aware about noticing when someone makes your day, thank them to reinforce what they did, and learn from that. Make Someone's Day is also about doing unexpected, unplanned acts of kindness that help in a significant way and make a world of difference. That's the magic. Make Someone's Day can be done in so many ways, including online as well as in person, for people you know or for strangers you've never met but could use a lift.

What better way to learn than through the simple VIP Model introduced in chapter two that has people feeling like a VIP? You'll learn simple and more detailed ways you can make someone's day at work, at home, with family, and in a crisis. You may discover that you have already made someone's day in many ways without even realizing it. Giving your spouse, significant other, close friend, or colleague a hug, a smile, some flowers, or a show of support when they need it—that's part of it. Unexpected acts of appreciation that come in the right way and at the right time.

You'll find chapters filled with stories and examples of how people made someone's day along with illustrations of actions you can take that are comfortable for both introverts and extroverts. You'll learn about the neuroscience of making someone's day, the anonymous ways you can make someone's day, and the power of making someone's—or even saving someone's—life. In the last chapter, you have several different forms you can use to track your experiences and grow your skills. For more examples and stories or to share yours, go to makesomeonesdaybook. com or howardhprager.com or our Facebook page to read and see more examples and share your stories and experiences.

HOW TO USE THIS BOOK

This book can be read and used in a number of ways. Read it cover to cover and get many ideas of what you and others can do to make someone's day. Read a chapter or example at a time, and try it out—see how it feels for you to do. Does it feel natural? Is it something you can do again? Pick this book up when you need to pick up your employees, colleagues, teammates, or even yourself—by making someone's day.

This introduction has provided several examples of *make someone's day* experiences. They can happen when you least expect it and in ways that are unforgettable throughout your life. Each chapter will provide new insights and examples as to how you can make someone's day in different situations as a leader, as a manager, and as a thoughtful person. Each chapter ends with a short summary and quick action you can take to apply *make someone's day* **immediately**. If you do this in each chapter, you'll be on your way to becoming a master by the time you've finished the book.

PUTTING INTO PRACTICE

Before you read any further, find the address, phone number, or email of at least one person who made your day or even your life. Contact them however you like and say thank you. There's actually a later chapter on this, but why wait? Do it now. Then come back and read on!

Chapter one shares more examples and five key reasons *why* to make someone's day.

CHAPTER 1

· ·

WHY YOU NEED TO
MAKE SOMEONE'S DAY!

"If you want to feel good, go out and do some good." —Oprah Winfrey

WHY GO OUT OF our way, even in a small way, to make someone's day? It brings us closer together, inspires us, and people and teams become more productive, energized, and happy.

Here are several key reasons. First, it feels good. Second, it's the right thing to do. Third, you get to know that you positively affected someone's life in a meaningful way—it's significant and important for others at a particular time. Fourth, even small acts can have a memorable impact. Fifth, it affects everyone in their own way.

Let's start by looking at what we're already doing. We often make someone's day and don't even realize it; that's how easy it is to do.

FIVE KEY REASONS TO MAKE SOMEONE'S DAY

First, it's surprisingly simple. Making someone's day doesn't need to take much effort. A smile, a nod, or simply a helping hand can make a huge difference for someone—even you—when they're feeling down or not acknowledged, they need some help, or they just need a friendly face. How do you feel when someone smiles at you when you're sad or lost in thought? Often better, right? How many times has someone said a simple greeting and lifted your spirits? That wave or hello from a manager, leader, colleague, or even a stranger can bring a smile to your face when you might need one. How often have you been stuck trying to figure out what to do or where to start on a project or assignment but can't get unstuck? A smile or wave may be all you need.

Ever run to catch a train or bus and the conductor or driver sees you, waves, and waits a couple of extra seconds so you can catch your ride before it pulls away? Maybe not as often as you'd like, but occasionally. These two examples don't take much effort but could make a big difference to someone on a schedule trying to get going, make it to work, an appointment or just get home. These are simple examples of actions that can make someone's day.

Second, if you're the one making someone's day, it comes back to you. There is an uplifting feeling you get back when you make someone's day. Chapter 3: The Neuroscience Behind It, explains what happens in the brain when you make someone's day and the mirror effect you experience when they say, "You've made my day." Talk about a great "return on investment."

Third, words of kindness and praise lift us up. We don't get or give praise often enough in life. That's a shame, because it costs nothing to do and feels great to receive. Here's a common example. Have you ever been in a hospital or doctor's office and received help from a nurse, technician, orderly, or assistant staff? Chances are they don't get much appreciation. Everyone wants to hear what the doctors have to say. These dedicated frontline healthcare workers are often backline and secondary in the minds of patients and families, but they're actually the ones providing the most care. By taking time to acknowledge their efforts—as a patient or visitor—you lift their spirits and make their day. That acknowledgement of appreciation can roll over to the care of other patients by a healthcare worker who feels uplifted. And if you're a healthcare worker, seeing a patient or a family member's smile, thanks, or acknowledgement can make your day and give you a lift, especially because you don't expect anything in return for what you do.

When Alan compliments his nurses in his cancer treatment, he leaves feeling more joyous and in a better place at a time when he should be struggling and in pain. His nurses became more perky and cheerful whenever he comes in for treatment. During the COVID-19 pandemic, every frontline medical worker put themselves at risk of infection to help patients. It was a beautiful thing to see people in major cities such as London and New York clapping and applauding their efforts every day after work during the pandemic.

The people most companies put on the frontline are the lowest paid, have the highest turnover, and are least appreciated. They get the complaints from your most important people—your customers. They too should also be applauded. You want them to treat your customers exceptionally well, in which case you need to treat them well. Richard Branson, the Virgin entrepreneur, has written books on how he works hard to take care of his employees, because they take care of his customers. Make their day and they will make yours, your customers', and your company's!

Fourth, even small acts of kindness can make big differences. When I switched seats on a plane so a couple who were sitting apart could be together, they were most grateful. It was easy for me to do, and when I looked over, they were smiling and holding each other's hand. This happened to me, too. I was sitting in the middle seat and the woman sitting next to me on the aisle said, "Let's change seats. You're so much taller than me and need the room." That simple act made my day (and a more comfortable flight). There are so many opportunities to make someone's day happen when traveling; we just need to take the time to notice and do it. Pilots and gate staff, think of what you can say or do for the flight attendants and passengers waiting to board your plane. Flight attendants, see what you can do to make someone's day for your passengers, and it will come back to you and your airline, too. Here's what Jody did for some flight staff. In Chicago, Garrett's popcorn is delicious and well known with outlets in the city and at the airports. Jody bought a couple of small bags and gave them to the flight attendants as she boarded her flight as a spontaneous thank-you for their work. You can imagine how cheerful they were the whole flight! She made their day, and they in turn made the day for everyone on that flight.

Fifth, it affects everyone in their own way and at different times. One time a smile may be all that is needed to make someone's day; at other times it takes more effort. You don't necessarily know. You need to use your emotional intelligence and intuition to figure out what may be needed. Think of it like cooking with a new recipe. Sometimes it takes a while to figure out the right proportion of ingredients or what else you need to add to the recipe to get it just right. And sometimes your recipe may taste better one time than it will at another time. It's hard to get everything perfect every time (although we hope our favorite restaurants do). Make Someone's Day is the same way. Sometimes a smile, greeting, or compliment works magic, and other times something else does the trick. Be flexible. If possible, know the person whose day you're trying to make as best you can and assess the situation. But like a good recipe, we all know when we've got it right! For example, my recipe with parents is to say something positive about their kids. They don't hear that enough, and when you genuinely tell them, they appreciate it so much. My recipe with workers is to be specific when I thank them so they know what they did was most helpful.

So how do you start? Always keep Make Someone's Day at the forefront of your mind. Put it on your to-do list, think about it on your way to work, or think about it even when you're working out. Open yourself up to notice the world around you. It does take awareness and some emotional intelligence to spot potential opportunities to make someone's day. We don't always know the right thing to do, but like dipping your toe in the water, you'll know when it feels right. And the more you try and the more it works, the better you feel and the more you'll use it. That's how you make it a habit, and when you do, you'll be rewarded with your success.

I'm a morning person and love to greet people warmly in the morning with a cheery hello and some conversation. Sometimes that's just what others need to make their day. Sometimes not. Maybe it's all you can do to feed your family, get lunches made, and get people and you out the door in the morning and you have no greeting left in you. Or if you're not a morning person, you grumble at those that are too cheerful, as I discovered when I got a new colleague and tried being my cheerful morning self with her. It didn't take me long to realize I'd get a better response if I chatted with Kathryn later in the morning than first thing.

We need to know what people need and when they need it. We all have our routines to get ourselves going before we start our day. Why do you think the barista at your favorite Starbucks or coffee shop knows your drink so well if you're a regular? Yet even when we're at our busiest or sleepiest, we can offer a smile, a kind word, or an acknowledgement of others that can make their day, and ours.

Commuting is often a great time to make someone's day, and if you're not commuting, walking in the neighborhood can provide the same idea. I pay attention to what's going on around me as I walk, ride, travel, or enter online meetings when working remotely. I lend a hand if needed, offer a smile to someone who looks like they can use it, or join the meeting both prepared and with a positive attitude. Sometimes I get lost in my own thoughts or am focused on what's ahead for me and my day. At those times I remind myself to stay aware of the world and situation unfolding around me. What might someone need or want—just a chance to talk with someone, a seat, an extra hand, a note taker, or a cheery greeting? A warm look or smile has often made my day and gotten me more centered and on the right track, and I try to do the same for others.

Walking into your workplace or signing online for that first meeting is a golden time to make someone's day. I love to greet people as I walk into my office or enter a Zoom meeting. Take a moment to think about how you want to be present as you enter the meeting. See how others respond. As the day progresses, other opportunities pop up. Make Someone's Day is not about being nice to everyone around you, although if everyone did that, can you imagine how powerful that would be? Make Someone's Day is about the one-on-one interactions we have both with strangers and with those we know well. It starts with doing something that may take very little effort from you but turns out to be the right thing at the right time for others. It's about what you naturally do and don't even think about—saying hello, chatting about the weather or last night's ballgame or how that customer's project is coming along. It's all about making a difference with others in such a way that it changes their day around by making their day and, as a result, improves yours as well. And think about the reputation you'll begin to have as a go-to person for inspiration and support!

Make Someone's Day is a matter of awareness. Being aware of how the people around you are acting, of who appears upset, distracted, or encumbered. Simply noticing, thinking, and acting on ways you can help make their day. I don't consciously think about "making someone's day" every moment. I think about how I can help or show some warmth, how I can connect or make a small difference for others that I come into contact with, and then it just happens. In the locker room at the gym sharing small talk with the person next to me, chatting with the receptionist at the front desk, waiting in line for an elevator or at a store, or getting to an online meeting early or staying on to connect with someone afterward: all are places we go and things we do routinely without a second thought. Two short examples. On a team call recently, I chatted with a colleague and asked how he was doing. "Fair," he replied. I asked if he'd like to talk afterward, and he said yes. I called after the meeting and helped him work through several concerns he had, making his day. Another example came when working out on Valentine's Day. The fitness instructor gave us all miniature chocolate hearts after class. (Maybe so we'd need to take a second class to work off the chocolate!) I gave mine to the receptionist at the front desk. He loved it. That was a spontaneous thought, easy to do, and much appreciated since receptionists are often forgotten. His appreciation made his day and mine. What can you do that easily if you put a little thought into it? Who might you share a treat with?

Here are some easy actions you can take to make someone's day.

- **Greeting colleagues and others with a nod, a cheery hello, a good morning.** This simple act is so unexpected in today's rushed world that it often makes someone's day.
- **Using someone's name.** The most magical sound in the world is someone saying our name, and correctly. What a nice feeling to be addressed in that way.
- **Helping carry a package.** Sometimes people need and accept the help, yet even if they don't, it's the offer that can make someone's day.
- **Lifting a suitcase up/down/in/out.** You can notice when someone is struggling with their bags, and coming to their aid is often appreciated.
- **Holding a door or elevator open a second longer when you see someone trying to catch it.** A simple act of courtesy that can help people get where they're going faster.
- **Offering the last seat/ticket to someone else.** This happened to me as I was desperately trying to get on a flight home that evening and another person said they had no problem waiting an extra hour for the next flight. He made my day and in this case got rewarded by the airline for doing so because he gave up his seat and got a voucher for future travel as well as a guaranteed seat on the next flight.
- **Taking your coworker or a neighbor to lunch.** You never know what connection they may be wanting, and even just the offering may make their day.
- **Shoveling or blowing your neighbor's driveway after you've done yours.**
- **Helping someone search for something lost or missing.** You can be a hero!
- **Remembering former teachers and letting them know the difference they made in your life.** No matter when or how long it's been, this is always appreciated.

- **Paying for coffee for the person/car behind you in line.** What a great surprise! Tasha had this happen to her driving through a Starbucks, and she was so lost in thought she just said thanks and drove off. She now frequently will pay it forward as she thinks about it when driving through Starbucks.

PUTTING INTO PRACTICE

This chapter highlighted five key reasons to make someone's day. 1) It feels good to do. 2) It's the right thing to do. 3) You get to know that you positively affected someone's life in a meaningful way. 4) Even small acts can make a big difference. 5) It affects everyone in their own way. Additional simple, everyday examples exemplify ways you can make someone's day. Start noticing how often that happens to you and by you in the course of a day.

What examples do you have of small things you regularly do that can make someone's day?

Stop now and think about the last person who smiled at you. How did that make you feel? Did anything bring that on? Who are you going to smile at when you're done reading? Make a mental note of who that is and see their reaction to your smile. Then choose one of the easy actions on the list on the previous page and make a plan to do one.

In chapter two, you'll learn the four simple steps to making someone's day that I call the Make Someone's Day VIP Model. Keep your own examples in mind as you read about each step.

CHAPTER 2

. . . .

THE FOUR EASY STEPS TO MAKING SOMEONE'S DAY

"You give but little when you give of your possessions. It is when you give of yourself that you truly give." —Kahlil Gibran, The Prophet

IT SEEMS LIKE EVERYTHING is easier to learn with some steps and a model. I believe in simple models. They can guide us and help us learn new concepts much easier. We're all familiar with recipes—they make cooking easier. Or simple math models like A + B = C or 2 + 2 = 4. I wanted a model for Make Someone's Day that was easy to use and easy to remember. Acronyms help us remember. In science, H_2O is water. Or in school I remember learning the KISMIF model: Keep it Simple, Make It Fun.

For Make Someone's Day, I've thought about the right acronym that would reflect on the process well. I realized that when you make someone's day, they feel like a VIP, a very important person. So that's what I've called it, the VIP Model. Plus I wanted to add some R&R so people could reflect about what they did. That's the model, VIP + R&R. Just four easy steps to help you learn how to make someone's day. And it's really the first three steps, the VIP, that are most important.

View & observe

Identify & determine

Plan & act

Reflect & review

The addition of R&R helps us think about what we did, what we learned, and how we may want to apply Make Someone's Day next time.

STEP 1: VIEW & OBSERVE

View and observe what's going on around you. When viewing and observing the world, you'll find opportunities pop up for you to make someone's day, whether in person or online.

Awareness is the key, awareness of people and situations or circumstances that are going on. What clues can you pick up? Are people rushed? Distraught? Do they look like they're in pain? Isolated? Ignored? Need help? Some of these may be indicators that they are open to someone making their day. If you're online, view and observe what friends or others are posting (or not) on social media as an indicator of how they're doing. It might lead you to take action to make their day depending on what they're saying or doing in person or what they're saying and describing in their posts online. In either case, online or in person, pay particular attention to people you work with, those who work for you, and those you are closest to.

STEP 2: IDENTIFY & DETERMINE

Based on your observations, identify what you think someone needs. A smile or helping hand? An idea or some funding? How about removing or lowering some barriers, real or imagined? Online, are people looking for a like or comment? Or a donation or some help? You'll identify some actions you can take in a split second; other actions may take more time for you to identify and figure out. In either case, making someone's day is a choice you make based on what you identify in your observations and then determine what to do.

In this step, you increase your awareness of what may be needed through attentive listening, emotional awareness, and insight and intuition. This leads you to identifying possible actions such as signing a petition, finding and returning a lost wallet, holding an elevator door open, lifting up a case or stowing luggage, or adding a comment depending on the situation. How about lending a hand or support for meeting a deadline with a work project or assignment or fixing something that's not working? Gauge the person's response after saying good morning or simply smiling as you walk by them. Use your observations and past experiences to try and figure out what actions may be helpful and what the person may think. You can have a second sense that someone may want a smile or greeting or if doing so would break their concentration and be an annoyance. Start with the simplest of actions like a smile, some praise, or appreciation, and work up from there.

If you're doing this online, be sure to like, comment, and even share posts that are of value. Expand the number of postings you see and read about, and as you do, comment or like them as appropriate. Keep safe online in doing so. Remember the person whose day you are making may not acknowledge it, especially online. That's okay, you're not doing it for that reason. My wife bakes challah bread every Friday, and I post the picture on social media because I'm so proud of the delicious tradition she started during COVID-19. And it's so funny how many people have told me they look forward to seeing what kind she creates each week. This has made me more aware of both the pictures I post and what I say about them when I do. Because I'm making someone's day by sharing them, even if they don't comment or say something.

STEP 3: PLAN & ACT

Plan your action and carry it out based on your observations and what you identify that others may need. Make Someone's Day isn't supposed to be hard or necessarily take a lot of effort. More often you'll find responding at the spur of the moment makes it all the more delightful and unexpected for others, the people you're helping.

Again, start simply. If you're in person and you think they could use some interaction, start with a glance, a look, a smile, and a kind word—see how they respond. That may just be enough interaction to make their day. Or they may give you a signal that they are open and interested in more of a connection or need your help. Then you figure out what they may need and how you can help them through a comment or question.

Think about a time you may have done something unintentionally but didn't realize it. That happened to me. Let me tell you when I didn't make someone's day. I took my Scouts to England, and we all stayed with families for home hospitality. The six-year-old granddaughter and grandson of the couple I stayed with came over to meet me. But Nicola was not happy after she met me. She went over to her grandma and said, "Nan, I wore my brand new dress and Howard didn't even say anything." Simply saying, "What a pretty dress," would have done the trick, especially since I didn't know it was new. That comment would have kept me out of hot water with Nicola. Complimenting others on new glasses, clothes, or hairstyles could make someone's day because it supports their decision or purchase they made. I'm glad to say Nicola got over that and we became friends. It helps when you're six!

When you take action, spontaneous or planned, the other person may or may not respond. Remember they may not necessarily say, "You made my day," or even thank you, but from their actions or expression, you'll know it mattered to them. A nod, a glance, or a smile directly from them to you shows they appreciated your comment or action and that it may have made their day. I was a bit stressed this week and turned on my favorite radio station, WDCB, and at that very moment, a tuba solo came on. As a tuba player, I was in my element, and it brought a smile to my face and joy to my ears and relaxed me. I called the radio station and told the DJ, "Your selection of what to play just made my day!" She was delighted and said it was great for her to hear that, and I in return made her day by saying so. That's a double win, because we both made each other's day. That simple interaction was all it took—a random song played on the radio and a thoughtful thank-you and comment and you're on your way!

Saying good morning to the security guard at the front desk of an office or building is easy. In return, I've made friends or learned something about them, their background, or that some special guests were visiting that day. I made their day with my morning greeting, and they made mine by sharing some insight or helpful information.

If online, start looking at your social media in a new way. If you just skim social media without interacting, find postings on social media you want to comment on and do so. Share your own posts and others that are meaningful to you. If you are already doing that, try doing so more often. When interacting online, don't necessarily expect a response; you may be setting yourself up for disappointment if you do. Feel good about posting or commenting on something you like. If you get a response back afterward, so much the better because you know then you've had an impact.

STEP 4: REFLECT & REVIEW

The first three steps are the action steps in Make Someone's Day. **R&R** is all about reflecting and reviewing your actions. What did your actions appear to do for the other person? Did you experience the boomerang effect? How did that make you feel?

These results determine how you'd like to make someone's day next time—do the same thing or try something different? What worked and why? What didn't work? It's as important to learn from what's not working. Keep improving how well and frequently you make someone's day. Make it a daily habit. It doesn't always work, but when it does, it's simply magical. Plus you can almost never go wrong from trying. That's what this fourth step does. It has you look back to go forward. Chapter fourteen provides several templates you can use to better track your efforts or create your own template. Tracking helps us continue to improve our efforts. And as Marshall Goldsmith says, if we measure it, we do it. Start measuring!

Too often when we do something for someone, even make someone's day, we expect a payback in some way such as an acknowledgement, a thank-you, a lead, a recommendation, or a referral. Don't expect anything!

Just feel good about what you did.

The biggest challenge with Make Someone's Day is that you want it to *always* work and for the boomerang effect to *always* happen. You set yourself up for disappointment with those expectations. When they don't say, "You made my day," or you don't feel the boomerang effect, you can feel let down. You may even question your own actions. Don't question your actions, and don't set expectations. Ask yourself was the intention there? Did you feel good? Did they smile back, nod, or look like they appreciated it? Realize maybe next time something will be said.

Start making someone's day regularly, because the more you do, the more frequently you'll hear those words and the sooner it can become a habit that you won't even think about, you'll do it regularly and naturally. As you start making a conscious effort to make someone's day, expand your comfort zone. Is liking something on social media too easy for you? Then start commenting or reposting comments and articles you like. Do you choose to limit your in-person connection to just a smile or nod? Then try some light banter. If you need to practice that, try doing it with some friends or family members first. The key is to continuously grow your practice of making someone's day.

Keep expanding and going further. Everyone wants to feel like a VIP sometimes. Be ready for some of your efforts not to work. The hardest feeling is when you try something and it backfires or you get no reaction or, even worse, a negative response. Make Someone's Day doesn't always work, and what works one time may not work at another time. Every person, every moment, every situation is unique. Remember that and you won't be disappointed. It works more often than not. You should get a reaction at least once every few times. And some of the times you don't, you can feel good knowing that you tried and will feel the benefit from doing the right thing.

MAKE SOMEONE'S DAY VIP MODEL

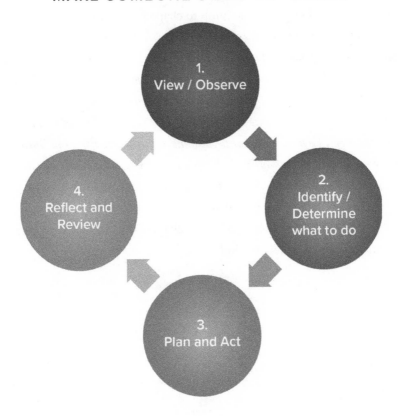

Isn't being treated like a VIP an experience we all want and sometimes envy those that get that treatment? You can give others the VIP treatment. That is a treat for them and for you. Then take a little time for some R&R. Reflect on what you did and on their reaction. Review what you might do differently next time. This is the best way to learn how to get better at Make Someone's Day.

PUTTING INTO PRACTICE

The Make Someone's Day VIP Model helps you become more aware of people around you and makes use of your emotional intelligence and observation skills to determine how to make someone's day. The four steps spell it out a little more specifically to make it easier to follow and track. To learn more about tracking, jump to chapter fourteen.

Practice can help you learn the VIP Model. To start, you may want to practice each step with a family member or close friend and share what you noticed. Check out your observations with them when you view and observe. Were you right? Then try the next step by confirming what you've identified and determined and get some feedback on that. Based on your feedback for the first two steps, then add the third: plan and act and actually do it. Then see the reaction you get and afterward take time to reflect and review. Like any muscle, it will take work to make it a part of who you are. Get started tonight with viewing and observing what's going on around you.

Now that we know how to do it, chapter three is all about *why* it works—the neuroscience behind Make Someone's Day.

CHAPTER 3

. . . .

THE NEUROSCIENCE
BEHIND IT

"You have brains in your head. You have feet in your shoes. You can steer yourself, any direction you choose." —Dr. Seuss

I THOUGHT A QUOTE from a doctor (!) would be a good way to start off this chapter as we get into the scientific perspective. Why does Make Someone's Day work? At its essence, it's the neurological effect that Make Someone's Day has on us and the people we are helping. Let me—and a few neurologists and doctors—simply explain what's happening when we make someone's day and why we feel uplifted, which I call the Boomerang Effect.

THE BOOMERANG EFFECT

The Boomerang Effect is my term for the reciprocal feeling you get when someone says to you, "You made my day!" I've seen many Make Someone's Day moments throughout my life, and the true key to it is the more we make someone's day, the more their appreciation for that action makes our day, too. Just think about that—what else has such a powerful two-way effect? Sir Isaac Newton would be smiling, having discovered that for every positive action there is an equal and opposite action in return.

That's what happens when you make someone's day: you benefit as well!

What does this boomerang effect do for you? Whatever you said or did to make someone's day was truly extraordinary for the other person. When they say, "You made my day," it isn't just a simple acknowledgement; it's a, "Wow, what a great impact you had on me when I needed it most!" You may already be starting to see from the examples I've shared that it may not take much effort for you to have an impact that changes someone's day or life around. Even simple and easy actions can have a great and even profound impact.

The boomerang effect happens to you immediately upon hearing the words, "You made my day." Your mirror neurons fire in your brain and you get a positive psychological rush. This lets you know that you are making a significant difference for someone while getting the boomerang benefit to boost your day, too. All of which encourages you to continue to find ways to make someone's day a regular part of your life.

THE COCKTAIL FOR YOUR BRAIN

When you make someone's day, they get a neurological "cocktail" that extends far beyond an endorphin rush. While endorphins play a role in our overall well-being by warding off pain and perpetuating pleasure, they alone do not create a rush or burst of happiness. Serotonin, oxytocin, and dopamine mixed with the endorphins are the "cocktail" that truly makes us happy and makes your brain feel good.

According to Eva Ritvo, MD, "Neuropeptides are the tiny molecules that allow neurons to communicate. They facilitate messages to the whole body when we are happy, sad, angry, depressed, or excited. These feel-good neurotransmitters—dopamine, oxytocin, and serotonin—are all released when a smile flashes across your face, for example. This not only relaxes your body, but it can also lower your heart rate and blood pressure. Each time you smile at a person, their brain coaxes them to return the favor. You are creating a relationship that allows both of you to release feel-good chemicals in your brain, activate reward centers, make you both more attractive, and increase the chances of you living longer, healthier lives." That's powerful, and just from a smile. What's not to like? And how does this happen?

When you make someone's day, this trigger impacts our brain in many positive ways through empathy and mirror neurons. According to Ritvo, "There are structures in the brain that are dedicated to helping you see things from the perspectives of others, so these mental processes get some great exercise when you put yourself in the shoes of another person and try to give them what they need." Which is what you are doing with Make Someone's Day, seeing things from the other person's perspective and determining what they may need.

BEING KIND MATTERS

Dr. Ritvo is also the author of the book *Bekindr* and founder of Bekindr, an organization that promotes the transformative power of kindness. This description on their website begins to identify the boomerang effect: "Humans are social animals, so it is no surprise that we are wired to help one another. There are many ways to give, and the good news is that we now understand that both the giver and receiver benefit from the relationship. Neuroscience has demonstrated that giving is a powerful pathway for creating more personal joy and improving overall health."

Dr. Elisha Goldstein wrote *The Now Effect: How a Mindful Moment Can Change the Rest of Your Life*. She discusses the mirroring of others' behavior. She calls it emotional contagiousness and says it has a direct effect on how the people around us feel. According to Goldstein, everything you do matters because "the way people behave is contagious and causes a ripple effect across friends of friends of friends. Like a wave in the ocean ripples out and causes movement around it, so do people's emotions cause a ripple with others. It's why when others are happy, we can be happy, when others are anxious, we get more anxious, etc." When you're in a good mood, it is a great time to activate make someone's day. Take advantage of your positivity and help others be in a good mood. The more often you make someone's day, the bigger the ripple effect it can have and then impact even more people as they feel good and pass it on. Keep making those ripples larger.

I had the chance to work with baseball hall of famer Ernie Banks, who was a big believer in networking and called his keynote talk "A Friend of Your Friend is My Friend." He was all about helping one another. Relationships are not just limited to the two people directly in them but include the contacts each one of us has. That's how LinkedIn works as well. "Working much like the 'Six Degrees of Separation' concept, you start by connecting with those you know and who know you, and through them build a larger network for the purpose of gaining resources, finding freelance work or clients, and building alliances and partnerships. You have an opportunity, through your contacts, to reach their contacts and expand your network," according to Randy Duermyer in *Balance Small Business*.

Psychiatrist Dr. Anna Yusim talked with me about a study on money and making someone's day. "Elizabeth Dunn, Associate Professor at the University of British Columbia and co-author of the book *Happy Money*, conducted a series of studies and found when we help others, it makes us even happier than we expect. She began by handing out cash to students on campus. She told some students to spend it on themselves and others to spend it on someone else. Those who spent money on other people were happier than those who treated themselves. Moreover, those who spent it on themselves showed a higher stress response and greater feelings of shame."

Think about how you feel giving specific presents to people on birthdays and special occasions. Especially if you put time into thinking and choosing the right gift, aren't you as excited or even more when they too are pleased with what you got them? Now think about how people feel when you spend money on someone who doesn't have much. Chapter seven talks about the buy-nothing project where people donate items they don't have any more use for so others can benefit. Helping others in need is a Make Someone's Day moment.

Understanding and empathizing with what another person is going through helps guide you to identify and plan how to make their day. Empathy enables you to understand what others have been or are going through. The more you can understand what they need, the more you can do what's needed to make their day. As you do, you receive more of the boomerang effect. And the more you do, the more you want to do.

Dr. Robin Banerjee, Professor of Developmental Psychology at the University of Sussex, and graduate student Jo Cutler conducted research to show that being kind and caring about others can actually make us genuinely happy in a number of different ways. "We know that deciding to be generous or cooperating with others activates an area of the brain called the striatum. This area responds to things we find rewarding, such as nice food and even addictive drugs. The feel-good emotion from helping has been termed 'warm glow' and the activity we see in the striatum is the likely biological basis of that feeling." Further research in psychology shows the link between kindness and well-being is with us throughout life starting at an extremely young age, under two. And for adolescents, even reflecting on having been kind in the past may be enough to improve a teenager's mood.

Why does kindness make us so happy? Banerjee and Cutler have identified five different mechanisms that make us feel good, depending on our personalities. These are covered throughout this book: smiling, connecting with others, being kind, the boomerang effect of kindness, and righting a wrong. Let's learn more.

"Helping others is often a highly social activity, which creates a beautiful cycle of smiling. When you smile the whole world smiles with you because you are triggering the other person's mirror neurons, impacting the brain in a positive way. A key theory about how we understand other people in neuroscience suggests that seeing someone else show an emotion automatically activates the same areas of the brain as if we experienced that emotion for ourselves," Banerjee and Cutler write. For example, haven't you found yourself laughing just because someone else is? Smiling and laughing is contagious. They activate your mirror neurons.

KINDNESS WORKS WITH YOUR EMOTIONS

It works with other emotions, too, from joy to sadness. You feel joyous when you hear good news about someone you care about and are saddened when you hear the opposite. Maybe the old saying, "Laugh and the world laughs with you, but cry and you cry . . ." well, not alone but with others, too. As Banerjee and Cutler write, "This is especially powerful for people we are close with, such as close friends and family, as our representations of them in the brain physically overlap with our representations of ourselves. Doing a kind act to make someone we care about who is sad feel better also makes us feel good, partly because we feel the same relief they do and partly because we are putting something right." This includes helping them overcome their negative or down feeling and making them feel better, supported, and uplifted.

Banerjee and Cutler add, "Most people would like to think of themselves as kind, so acts of kindness help us to demonstrate that positive identity and make us feel proud of ourselves. In one recent study, even children in their first year of secondary school recognized how being kind can make you feel 'better as a person . . . more complete,' leading to feelings of happiness. Research has shown that being in a good mood can make you even more kind." Being kind, being in a good mood, mirroring others feelings, these all come together when you make someone's day.

BENEFITING OTHERS WITHOUT DIRECT FACE-TO-FACE CONTACT

What about for introverts and philanthropists? As mentioned earlier, research shows that spending extra money on other people may be more powerful in increasing happiness than spending it on yourself. "This can even apply to humanitarian problems such as poverty or climate change," Banerjee and Cutler say. "Getting engaged with charities that tackle these large-scale issues provides a way to have a positive impact on them, which in turn improves our mood." What a powerful effect, impacting society and our planet and impacting you, too. This is why many people like to work for or volunteer with nonprofits. They empathize with the cause and want to contribute to the betterment of people and our planet. Contributing or volunteering to these causes also allows us to strengthen existing relationships and build new ones, creating new connections with people who care about the same things we do.

SUNSHINE HELPS TOO

Getting some sunlight is something that can help everyone while making people's day and more. Being in the sun minimally five to fifteen minutes a day, two to three times a week generally makes people feel good, and there are many scientific reasons for this effect, according to the newsletter *Medical News Today* in November 2020: "Exposure to UVB rays causes human skin to produce beta-endorphins, which are hormones that reduce pain. Their other benefits include:

- promoting a sensation of well-being and improving mood
- boosting the immune system
- relieving pain
- promoting relaxation
- helping wounds heal
- helping people feel more alert
- increasing job satisfaction when a person's workplace has access to sunlight
- reducing depression."

Offices and spaces with access to sunlight can make a difference all by itself. That's an easy way to make someone's day. Let's look at other ways how Make Someone's Day can help with stress and depression.

HELPING WITH STRESS

Stress is a reaction many of us struggle with. During stress, hormones like cortisol are released and our heart and breathing rates increase—the "fight or flight" response. Making someone's day can actually reduce stress. "All the great spiritual traditions and the field of positive psychology are emphatic on this point—that the best way to get rid of bitterness, anger, rage, or jealousy is to do unto others in a positive way," according to Stephen G. Post, a professor of bioethics at Case Western Reserve University School of Medicine. "It's as though you somehow have to cast out negative emotions that are clearly associated with stress—cast them out with the help of positive emotions."

My dad did that all the time. Instead of getting angry at an annoying driver, he'd look over and smile. Why get worked up over someone else's actions? It relaxed and destressed him, and just maybe it helped to lower the aggressive behavior of the other driver. According to Jeanie Lerche Davis in the article "The Science of Good Deeds" on WebMD, "When we smile or engage in good deeds, we reduce our own stress—including the physiological changes that occur when we are stressed."

Too much stress can lead to bigger problems. "If this stress response remains 'turned on' for an extended period, the immune and cardiovascular systems are adversely affected—weakening the body's defenses, making it more susceptible to abnormal cellular changes," Post explains on WebMD. "These changes can ultimately lead to a downward spiral—abnormal cellular changes that cause premature aging. It has been shown repeatedly that depression weakens your immune system, while happiness on the other hand has been shown to boost our body's resistance." Boost your resistance through being kind, positive, and happy, lower your stress, and share that feeling with others by making someone's day.

Depression and weakened immune systems aren't the only challenges. "Studies of telomeres—the end-caps of our genes—show that long-term stress can shorten those end-caps, and shortened end-caps are linked with early death," Post tells WebMD. "These studies indicate that we're dealing with something that's extremely powerful. Ultimately, the process of cultivating a positive emotional state through prosocial behaviors—being generous—may lengthen your life. Two large studies found that older adults who volunteered reaped benefits in their health and well-being. Those who volunteered lived longer than non-volunteers. Another large study confirmed this and found a forty-four percent reduction in early death among those who volunteered a lot—a greater effect than exercising four times a week," Post reports. Be sure to volunteer, but don't think you can just stop exercising because you do!

Harvard psychiatry associate professor Gregory Fricchione is working on a book about brain evolution and the development of human altruism. "If it is evolutionarily beneficial for human beings to benefit from social support, you would expect that evolution would provide the species with the capacity to provide social support," he tells WebMD. "This is where the human capacity for altruism may come from." Indeed, oxytocin may be connected to both physical and emotional well-being, says Fricchione. "Oxytocin is the mediator of what has been called the 'tend-mend' response, as opposed to the 'fight-flight' response to stress. When you're altruistic and touching people in a positive way, lending a helping hand, your oxytocin level goes up—and that relieves your own stress." There are so many psychological, emotional, and physical reasons to reduce stress and help others by making someone's day.

PUTTING INTO PRACTICE

There are numerous neurological benefits to being positive, volunteering, and supporting others. Smile, be kind, connect with others, right a wrong, and watch for the boomerang effect of the mirror neurons so that you feel good, too. Live longer and happier by volunteering and helping others, whether you're young or old. Take advantage of the natural drugs your body produces while doing good in the world through volunteering, altruism, and making someone's day.

Think about the last time you volunteered. Think back to the time and situation and decide if it made your day. Not all volunteer experiences make someone's day, so if you need to think of another situation, do so. When you think of the right situation, ask yourself these questions: Who were you with, what did you do, and how did you feel afterward? Write down those feelings. Then make a plan on when you will repeat that volunteer experience or do something similar and see if you get similar results.

Make Someone's Day starts with easy actions we can take without thinking about them.

CHAPTER 4

. . . .

THE EASIEST OF
ACTIONS TO TAKE

"Sometimes your joy is the source of your smile, but sometimes your smile can be the source of your joy." —Thich Nhat Hanh

WHAT'S ONE OF THE easiest, most universal actions to show friendliness? Smiling. We've talked about a smile as both something easy to do and the powerful neurological benefits you gain when you smile. It's such a recognizable action even if you don't speak the same language, people respond positively. Think about that for a moment. That's remarkable, really, a display of openness and warmth that everyone understands, knows, and likes. Travel writer Clemens Sehi uses a smile to set a friendly tone with strangers abroad: "When traveling, there is one thing that one realizes quite fast: a smile can change everything. It can open doors and the hearts of other people whose culture you do not even know." This happened to my sister Merril and I when we were backpacking through Europe after college. We were in Florence trying to find an affordable pensione to spend a few days. Giovanna opened her door with a smile but was suspicious of a man and woman travelling together. As soon as I smiled and pointed to Merril and said, "Sister," and showed her our passports, she welcomed us into her home, talking

43

nonstop every night, to which we could only smile, nod, and repeat the last few words in Italian. That was all she wanted. She made our day with her warmth, a lovely place to stay, and a good breakfast each morning.

Many business travelers have discovered the old saying, "You can win more friends with honey than with vinegar." They know a smile and a kind word with frontline workers at the check-in desk at the airport, rental car, hotel, or restaurant can make a big difference in how they are treated. No platinum status needed.

A smile, a friendly nod, or a helping hand may be all it takes to make someone's day. You are connecting with someone in the easiest of ways, words not even necessary. It shows warmth and connection. And it makes you feel better for doing it because others frequently smile back, nod, or give you a thumbs-up, in person and online. Sometimes that leads to a little conversation or chat. Saying hello and smiling to the receptionist when you walk into your office or a client can make you more welcome in their eyes.

On a call? Smiling is something that comes through whether you are seen or not. One of my first work projects was revising a brochure called "Your Voice is Allstate" so that everyone knew the benefit of smiling when talking to a customer. Whether wearing a mask in person or on the phone, be sure to emphasize a cheerful tone and inflection to ensure that people hear your smile.

A smile doesn't commit you to anything more than acknowledging the other person. I've often been lost in thought or struggling to resolve a work issue, and when I look up and make eye contact and see another person smiling at me, it relaxes me and eases my tension. It gives me a fresh perspective and energy. I hope when I've smiled at others, they've felt the same way. Let's look at why.

According to the article "There's Magic in Your Smile" by Sarah Stevenson in *Psychology Today*, a smile (and laughter) lifts our mood as well as the moods of those around us. Smiling activates the release of neuropeptides that work toward fighting off stress. A smile is contagious and can make us appear more attractive to others, burns off calories, and has many health benefits.

With all of these benefits, we should be smiling more often! When we smile at someone and they smile back, we feel more connected and less isolated. How do you feel when you smile at someone and they smile back at you? Think about that for a moment. It often can lead to people opening up to you. Smiling at work can relax people, de-stress a situation, and lead to new ideas and resources. When I've met people at the water cooler or in the lunchroom, a smile or hello has led to more of a connection and helpful information I may not have known otherwise. Have you experienced this?

In 2018, NBC News did a story on the benefits of smiling. "What's crazy is that just the physical act of smiling can make a difference in building your immunity," says Dr. Murray Grossan, an ENT (Otolaryngologist) from LA. "When you smile, the brain sees the muscle [activity] and assumes that humor is happening." This relaxes you and produces more good chemicals. Meetings can sometimes be deadly, but a shared glance or smile with a colleague can relax you, bring you into focus, and raise your engagement. And humor in a meeting with a joke or pun at the right time can get a reaction (chuckle or groan) from everyone and bring a renewed energy to the meeting. (Us punsters know when we've hit the mark when we get a good groan!)

Think of the opposite. Have you ever shaken hands or greeted someone who wasn't smiling? Did you ask yourself, "Are they sincere? Are they genuine? Do they care about me?" In business, smiles can open doors, open minds, and open thinking. The absence of it leads to doubt and less trust.

I was working intensely with Donna, one of my favorite faculty at the graduate school. We were designing a new customer service program, brainstorming together, and getting frustrated that the program hadn't completely jelled yet. We stopped, looked at one another, and both smiled, which brought us back with renewed focus on our client's needs. This opened the door to getting really creative, and as a result, we developed an award-winning customer service leadership program. Donna made my day through her smile, breaking our frustration at the time and allowing us to make our client's day by designing an outstanding program.

"Smiling is contagious not just because of how a smile looks from the outside, but also because of the intention and the feeling that is put behind a smile," says Jasmine Wang, communications manager at Smile Train, a charity providing corrective surgery for children with cleft lips and palates. A smile is also something you want to pass along. It makes you happier, and you want to share the good feelings it brings with others.

Researchers at the University of Kansas found that smiling helps reduce the body's response to stress and lowers your heart rate in tense situations. Another study linked smiling to lower blood pressure, while still another suggests that smiling leads to greater longevity. These all build on the studies reported in the last chapter on the neuroscience of making someone's day. Are you smiling yet? ☺

A GREETING, COMMENT, OR SHORT CONVERSATION

A greeting or simple comment can also make someone's day. Conversations, whether it's about the weather, sports, or life, can have an impact far beyond the mere acknowledgement of others. "Small talk" works best when communicating about a current event or simply the weather. That's nice, but how does it make someone's day? Step one of the Make Someone's Day VIP Model is viewing/observing the world around you. A brief conversation can provide more information by checking out what you observed and confirming if you were right. Then you can identify and plan your actions. I've gotten great information just by having a casual conversation with a receptionist and learning something to share with my client, making their day. One other tip: use the assistant or receptionist's name. Hearing one's name is magical, and by remembering it and doing so, you may just make their day, too. It can really be that simple—their name, a smile, and a friendly short chat and you've moved to the top of the list of people they want to help, because you made their day and in turn they want to help you.

Other benefits can come back to you from short conversations, such as appreciating something you hadn't known or getting ahead quickly when time is short. Have you waited in lines only to learn you needed to have something first (a number, a letter, a signature, money) before getting to the front? So frustrating, and yet a short conversation can clear that up right away and give you the information you need to either continue waiting or come back with the right documents. When I was at the University of Michigan, my friend John would say, "If you see a line, stand in it, because it's probably something you need to do." Often, he was right.

This example combines a smile, a short conversation, and even a surprise ending for Angela and Jake. "Our son was born premature with weak lungs, and his first sixty days of life were in the NICU (Neonatal Intensive Care Unit). During COVID-19, each visitor had to check in and complete screening questions prior to entering the hospital. One day as we approached the check-in desk, the staff person smiled and said, 'I know you both—Jake and Angela, correct? I know you are here every day visiting your son in the NICU. Here, I have your name badges all ready,' she said with a smile. In the sea of people who came through that hospital door and to be noticed and remembered with such a warm greeting, and for them to know why we were there absolutely made our day. From that point on, that staff member made sure our name badges were ready every day to help expedite our visit with our son, even leaving them for her replacement when she was not there." This remarkable story has a surprise ending. "Before Lawrence was discharged, Patty (we learned her name) gave Lawrence a gift—his first swim suit and enrollment in a water babies class when he is old enough. In the card, Patty wrote, 'You both have inspired me with your love and dedication to your little man.' To receive a gift and recognize our commitment to our precious baby made our day again and encouraged us immensely as new parents. We'll be eternally grateful."

When I see a colleague sad or frustrated, I strike up a conversation to see if I can help them. If I can, I empathize with them by sharing how I understand and may have experienced the same situation. I then share something I learned in dealing with this situation, and if it can help them, I often hear that I made their day. This could get them unstuck or at the very least let them know they are not alone and that they are supported.

Recently, I was waiting at the doctor's office, and a woman (I assume the mom) was with her high school–aged son for what appeared to be a routine physical. The mom was very anxious and frustrated. She felt her son was not taking things seriously. I saw a typical but nice teenager who just wanted to do stuff on his phone and not be tethered to his mother. When I saw him talking to the nurse before he went in to see the doctor, he was very polite to her. So when the son and nurse left to go in for the doctor's appointment, I mentioned to the mom that I thought her son was a very polite teenager. She looked up at me and said I made her day because she was so worried how he was coming across. Just let people know when you observe something positive.

Greeting the security guards or receptionists in a warm way at many office buildings can brighten both of your days. I made some good friends with the security guards at my first job. Many were graduate students at a nearby college. Even though they were just short conversations, they started off my day with a smile and good feeling. I made stronger friendships with several and stayed in touch after they left, even visiting Carlton and his wife Dottie in Belgium where they had moved. What a treat that was! At night, a conversation or comment on your way out is a chance to positively affirm a good day or lessen the impact of one not so good. Tomorrow is a new day. Who do you see first thing in the morning and how do you greet them? What about when you're leaving? And think about this online as well as in person.

According to the website Study-body-language.com, "It's important for us as social animals to look for some common ground with those who surround us—we want to feel part of a group so we can be accepted and understood." This leads to us mirroring the behavior of those around us. This is why we copy each other's body language, and it's why we feel chemistry and rapport with others. One example is when we get in an elevator. We turn around, face the front, and look at the lights that indicate the floor. We don't look at each other. Have you ever smiled at someone getting in an elevator? Started a conversation? It can seem strange because it's not common. People typically don't do that; we just get in, face the front, and watch the floor numbers light up. One style of a short talk is known as an elevator speech, because you've got the other person "captive" with you during the elevator ride, often only about thirty seconds. Why not bring the elevator speech to the elevator?! It's a good way to practice short conversations and even make someone's day before they get to their floor through a casual conversation. And if it's a boss or a CEO, what a great opportunity to update them on your project. At busy times, sometimes just holding the elevator for another person trying to catch it can make their day—an act of kindness in a frenzied world. After all, life has its ups and downs! (I confess I cannot write a whole book without at least one pun! Did that make you groan or smile? Good!)

Have you ever been stuck in a long security line at the airport or elsewhere when you're running late and are very short on time? It took me over three-and-a-half hours to get to Newark Airport from New York City on a pre-pandemic trip. I had given myself four hours to get there from my hotel, thinking that it only took me an hour to get to the city when I arrived so that should be plenty of time to check in and relax before my flight. Given how tight my time frame now was, I had a fair amount of anxiety with less than a half hour to get through security and to my gate before the flight left, and I assumed the doors would be closed even sooner. I couldn't miss this flight because I was coordinating with people flying in from three other locations. When I got to the security line, I mentioned to the security agent that my flight was boarding at that time. She and the people in line kindly (mostly) let me move to the front of the line. I made it through security, ran to the gate, and just made my flight—I was the last one to board before they closed the door. Phew. Now I don't recommend trying this yourself or making a habit out of this, but it's nice to know people can be understanding when you most need it. That made my day because otherwise I'd have had to scramble and make a lot of calls to figure out how to connect with the people I was going to meet. Frantic and harried times are when we need someone to make our day the most!

USE COMPLIMENTS

Compliments are one of the most special moments of life. Compliments derive from taking notice of praiseworthy situations and efforts. They create so much positive energy that things happen almost as if by magic afterward. As Sanjay Gupta, MD, said on CNN, "Compliments are a good way to make someone feel good and for you to feel good. Receiving a compliment is as much a social reward as being awarded money. The same area of the brain, the striatum, is activated with both a compliment and with cash." It's a lot cheaper to give a compliment! I find it amazing that it can be just as powerful as money, don't you? Compliments motivate people, increase happiness, show respect and admiration, and create a positive environment of gratitude and hope. One of my favorite authors, psychologist Dr. Leo Buscaglia, said, "Too often we underestimate the power of a touch, a smile, a kind word, a listening ear, an honest compliment, or the smallest act of caring, all of which have the potential to turn a life around."

Giving intentional compliments is powerful. When you do, be genuine and specific. Saying, "Thanks," is okay. Saying, "The article you wrote or shared is excellent and helped me to . . ." is more specific. And in doing so, it encourages others to repeat that action or behavior. Senders benefit from knowing that what they did mattered. And both online and in person, it's so easy to share an article that may be of interest or relevant to someone. People strive to do more of what they get complimented for. Don't you? Note to bosses: give more compliments, recognize your employees, and see chapter eight on making someone's day at work. It's not just money that will help retain and motivate your workers and associates!

It's always better to give the compliment directly, even online, when you can. Why? To show your sincerity and see the reaction. You can follow-up with a note so it becomes more formal, and if you're a boss, make sure it goes into the employee's record. An article on "The Art of the Compliment" by Hara Estroff Marano in *Psychology Today* reports, "Once praiseworthy situations are noticed, the awareness needs to be spoken. Recipients benefit from knowing that we notice and that we value them, and we also benefit from being givers of them." Receiving a compliment can encourage us to continue in the same direction. They can be strong motivators on a project or team. After all, who doesn't want to do more of something you get praised for? And when you give a compliment, you may receive the boomerang effect.

Compliments can be thought of as little gifts of love. They are not asked for or demanded. They tell a person they are worthy of notice. Compliments are a great way to acquire and practice social interaction skills because the returns are immediate. They foster a positive atmosphere and further communication and allow for better two-way exchanges. The more specific you can be and the closer to the actual event, the more people know what they are being complimented about and makes their day.

My brother-in-law, John, talks about the biggest of compliments, giving an award, while receiving a life lesson from a fifth grader. "Several years ago, I was selected to judge an essay contest for third, fourth, and fifth graders at the Carlos Fuentes Charter School in Chicago. Students were asked to write an essay to address the prompt, 'This I believe,' inspired by Carlos Fuentes' work, 'This I Believe . . . A Life From A to Z.' I awarded first prize to fifth-grader Jacqueline for her essay, 'This I believe . . . Beauty.' Her main idea was that beauty comes from within and that everyone is beautiful in their own way. In three moving, heartfelt pages, she lamented that too many people judge others solely by their appearance and encouraged readers to have confidence in their beauty. Most touching was the painful, personal experience she used to bring her points to life.

"When I met Jacqueline at the award ceremony, it was clear that no one would consider her pretty and that she knew it. But a few minutes of conversation convinced me that she was an amazing girl, which was exactly her point. After presenting the award, I told her how much her work moved me. 'You have a bright future,' I said. 'And you are beautiful, Jacqueline. Don't let anyone tell you differently.' Tears welled in her eyes as she thanked me. Jacqueline is likely in college now. I hope that in some small way I made her day, because her tears and essay certainly made mine."

Compliments can work if they are 1) sincere reflections of what we think and 2) given freely and not coerced. Compliments backfire if they are not genuine. Fake or ungenuine flattery disguised as a compliment is usually highly transparent. A false compliment makes the person who said it seem untrustworthy. It raises suspicions about what their motives really are, and that can undermine a whole relationship. Just be genuine when giving and getting them. And always say thank you (and you made my day, if they did).

SAYING THANK YOU

Saying thank you is the right way to acknowledge compliments. Too often we shrug them off when people tell us "nice work" or "good job" and instead say "not really" or "no" or "maybe." Receive compliments in the right way by acknowledging them and saying thank you. Even if you don't agree, just say thank you. Otherwise you're putting the person giving you the compliment in an awkward position. They may wonder, "Was I wrong? Did I say the wrong thing?" Show your appreciation and reinforce the giver of the compliment so they can feel good about what they said and continue to give compliments to you and others.

There are many benefits in giving compliments. First, focusing on and noticing the good qualities of the people around us gives our moods a boost. Second, a feeling of positivity is enhanced by compliments. The effects of positivity rebounds to us, creating a positive atmosphere. And third, it provides positive neurological impacts for the person doing it.

SUPER CUSTOMER SERVICE

When I get great help and service from another department, at a store, restaurant, really anywhere, I make sure to let others know. A most helpful Office Depot example comes to mind from the chair I'm sitting in. I work in my home office, including teaching classes that last for eight hours a day. I know lumbar support is important to my back and neck health so I don't lean forward constantly. When I mentioned this to the associate while shopping for a new desk chair, he recommended a chair that allows you to pull the back out at an angle so that when you're typing, you have greater support for your lower back. I love it and feel like it was one of the best purchases I've made for my home office. It's only because he asked and I said what I needed that the associate knew exactly what to recommend. And to my surprise, it was not the most expensive chair and in fact was cheaper than many others. He both made my day and made the sale!

I'm sure we all have stories about good customer service, people who took the time to listen, to understand, and to work to give you the answer you need or resolve a problem. That's because they're not commonplace. The customer service rep on the phone who stays with you the whole way to make sure your problem is solved, the sales clerk who looks up and down an aisle with you to find exactly what you need, and the front desk staff at the hotel who ensures you find your room in order and makes sure everything is right with your visit all are providing outstanding service. These special examples need to become more commonplace. Until then, I feel like I'm getting the VIP treatment when this happens, and it makes my day.

AVOID COMPLAINTS

The flipside of compliments is complaints, which is unfortunately much more common. Front desk or support people who quote you "the policy" instead of trying to find a solution can be frustrating and even maddening. The phrase that drives me most crazy is, "That's not my job." I always want to ask, "Whose job is it, then?" Sadly, we seem to complain or feel the need to complain much more often and all too frequently than we give compliments.

Compliments don't necessarily flow as easily as complaints, either. Why? We live in a society where people ignore others and, worse, complain about them. It's easy to complain about an assignment you don't like or to pick on people who are doing customer-facing work but not solving your problem. There's a reason customer service jobs have extraordinarily high turnover.

Complaints are part of what frontline workers have to deal with in their jobs. Complaints are so easy to make for a variety of reasons—you had to wait longer than you wanted, things didn't go as you expected, someone appeared to cut in front of you, etc. As I said in the last chapter, emotions are contagious, and that includes complaining. When you start complaining, others start doing so also. It's too easy to feel slighted and take it personally when that's not usually the case. Why do we complain so often and find it so easy to do?

First, negativity rewires your brain in that direction. Research shows that most people complain once a minute during a typical conversation. Second, complaining is tempting because it feels good, but complaining isn't good for you because it leads to more negativity. Much like positivity creates an uplifting atmosphere, complaining creates a negative atmosphere. Third, your brain loves efficiency and doesn't want to work any harder than it has to. Therefore, repeating a behavior, such as complaining, has your neurons branch out to each other to ease the flow of information. This makes it much easier to complain in the future, in fact so easily that you might not even realize you're doing it. And repeated complaining rewires your brain to make future complaining more likely. Over time, you'll find it's easier to be negative than to be positive, regardless of what's happening around you.

Complaining becomes your default behavior, which changes how people perceive you. Have you noticed there are people who just complain all the time, no matter what happens? Are those the people you want to be around and spend time with? Most importantly, don't be one yourself! Break that pattern and focus on the positive. You can stop this vicious cycle simply by not complaining and looking for ways instead to give a compliment.

When you see yourself in that downward complaining spiral, catch yourself and find something to compliment or be positive about. Make Someone's Day is about discovering and doing the small, simple things that can impact others in positive ways that are significant to them. It's giving you and your mind a break from the constant noise and clutter that surrounds our world. Stop wiring your brain to complain and instead rewire it to focus on giving and accepting compliments, smiling more, and sharing the benefits of making someone's day.

PUTTING INTO PRACTICE

It's easy to smile, give a compliment, and greet someone positively, in person or online. The health benefits and feelings you and the other person receive are significant. Avoid complaints and complainers when you can so they don't pull you down or, if you like a challenge, try to get them to see things in a positive light and make their day!

When was the last time you received customer service that was so good it made your day? What did you tell the person who did it for you? If you have a situation where you haven't thanked someone for doing it, go back and do that or send a note to the company or person. It's never too late to give someone a compliment and tell them they made your day!

Chapter five talks about how we need to show up and stand out, and when we do, we make someone's day.

CHAPTER 5

. . . .

SHOW UP AND STAND OUT

"There's nothing more daring than showing up, putting ourselves out there, and letting ourselves be seen." —Brené Brown

WHEN I THINK ABOUT what makes one successful in life, eighty percent of the effort is simply showing up, both in person and online. Whether searching for a new job and going on a job interview, attending a work meeting or project update, or getting together with a friend to work out, the simple act of showing up can make a world of difference in how others see you and lets you stand out. Showing up means being present, engaged, and involved. You gain nothing if you don't show up. When you do, it allows you to support others, provide input and ideas, demonstrate your commitment, and maybe even make someone's day. Professor Rosabeth Moss Kanter from Harvard Business School said in a *Harvard Business Review* article in 2013, "Being in the right place at the right time can make or break careers and companies."

I'm a long-time volunteer leader in my professional association, and I attribute my career success to my involvement in the Association for Talent Development (ATD). I am a past chapter and national leader because when they needed help, I stood up and volunteered. Whenever

I attend an association meeting now, I see old and new friends whose eyes light up upon seeing each other. Even virtually, there's a difference between those that show up for a webinar or program versus those that don't in terms of knowledge, insight, and information. You gain from being involved, whether it's learning something new, contributing your wisdom, or staying up to date. If my exercise classes don't have at least four people attending, they're cancelled. Everyone loses. Just show up!

Showing up at work sounds simple, and it is. We want a job and a paycheck. But how about once we walk inside the building or sign in to the VPN? What's our mindset and attitude? If you're asking yourself, "How can I do my best and make someone's day today?" you're on the right track. At the very beginning of the day, how we greet colleagues and associates can make their day, and they can make ours.

I'm an early riser and have always liked working early, and so did a colleague in another department. We'd exchange morning pleasantries (far easier to do if you're both extroverted and morning people). Her smile and comments, whether short and sunny or joking and jovial, always brought a smile to my face and helped make my day start off grandly. When working remotely, I find that first chat with someone sets the tone for the day. Whether you're online and talking by voice or sending a note in chat or greeting people in person, start with positive interactions and friendly comments.

TAKE ADVANTAGE OF SHOWING UP AND BEING FULLY PRESENT

It can be easy to start a conversation with something funny or something interesting in the news, the weather, or local sports. These are all topics that others can relate to. Okay, not my dad—he was good with a funny story or interesting news item but not sports. He looked at life with a positive attitude and cared greatly about his customers and family. His customers loved him for that and for working hard in their interests. I remember him driving orders to his customers on weekends if they were badly needed. Talk about showing up!

Be ready to make someone's day by giving the person you are speaking with your full attention. View/observe them—their words, tone, body language, and message—to help determine what they may need to make their day. If you need help online, Erica Dhawan's latest book *Digital Body Language* can help you make sense of what you're seeing and help you come across well, too. Identify and choose the action to take based on what you observed and then simply plan and carry it out. The VIP Model in action!

That first conversation of the day can be especially challenging when working remotely because we tend to jump right into our work or meetings like an on/off switch. If you work from home and have other family members working or schooling from home, make sure they are set up for success and good to go. Finish what you need to do with your family before jumping into your work and having a conversation with your boss, colleague, or client. I have a few places where I like to work from home depending on the weather, what meetings I have, and where my other family members are working. I also want to be able to share something newsy or informative so I look at the news headlines online to be able to make small talk or even inform others of something interesting that can affect their business. Once I'm set, I avoid distractions and give others my full attention to ensure I understand them completely, confirm what I heard, and respond appropriately. Following these guidelines may be all you need to make their day and get off to the right start.

MEETING THE NEEDS OF OTHERS

How you treat people always comes back to you in more ways than you can imagine and can lead to some great friendships and experiences, even when working virtually. It helps to be an extrovert who seeks this type of interaction, yet even introverts can find a colleague or friend to share greetings or confidences with and become better connected. In her book *Cultivate*, Morag Barrett talks about the need for all of us to have an ally at work. "Developing an Ally Mindset will help you to build and nurture your Ally Relationships." Her next book takes this concept further by exploring the importance of having a best friend at work. The best friend can be a supporter, a mentor, an advisor, or a colleague to share frustrations or joys with and to get clarification on work policies, processes, and assignments. These friends are also great for making sure you understand the jargon and acronyms that every organization has. In my first job, I turned to several friends/mentors to learn both the formal and informal rules, such as "always be typing when the Director walks by."

Get to know the people you work with and interact with the most. Discover their interests and hobbies. This isn't hard; just be observant as to their surroundings and what they like to talk about and do outside of work hours. Find *their* best time of day. The more you know about them and what motivates them, the easier it is to make their day. For example, my former colleague Susan loves hippos, and our former boss Kathy loves penguins. (No, I didn't work in a zoo!) Anything with those animals would bring a grin to their faces. When I saw a picture or small statue, I'd buy it for them. One CEO I worked for loved pigs. All his employees would buy pigs for him to the extent that when they moved offices, they had to build an extra-large cabinet for all the pigs! What does your boss or colleagues like? An animal, pet, color, location, or activity? Keep that in mind so you can make their day!

Bob talks about the time he was chief of staff for Ken Blanchard. As chief of staff, he did everything for Ken, including picking him up and dropping him off at the airport. They'd frequently chat about life on these drives. Ken was gone for three months on one trip to Europe. When he returned, Ken said, "I got something for you while I was away." He handed Bob a toy train from Sweden for his young son who loved trains. The fact that Ken thought about Bob and his young son on this long business trip absolutely made Bob's day. That inspired Dr. Bob and led him to his lifetime of work on motivating, recognizing, and rewarding employees.

Dr. Ron remembers the following story from his medical residency forty years ago. As a resident, he worked long and arduous hours. One night, needing to write up his reports, he basically collapsed in a chair at the nurses' station. His senior resident, Eric, recognized something wasn't quite right with Ron and asked if he had eaten dinner. Ron said no, he had too much work to do and was planning to subsist on his diet of coffee and peanut butter crackers found in the lounge, but Eric wouldn't have it. He could see Ron needed a break and more sustenance and then asked Ron, "Are your patients stable?" Ron answered, "Yes," and Eric then said, "Let's get to the cafeteria. The paperwork will be here when you get back."

Ron doesn't remember what he ate, but he does remember a colleague who cared about his physical and mental nourishment that a short dinner break provided for him that evening. Forty years later, Ron still recalls this story and said, "What Eric did that night was a simple, kind human gesture that made my day, became a touchpoint for my career, and reverberates with me all these years later."

MAKING MEETINGS AND INTERACTIONS MEANINGFUL

Many articles say we have too many meetings and that meetings are a waste of time. Poor meetings and meetings without agendas can indeed be a waste of time. A good meeting that's well run, values participants' input, provides an agenda with outcomes, and strives to be on time stands out. And you can make someone's day (or your team's day) by being a good listener, a good meeting leader, or a good participant. Encourage actions that keep your team on track. Speak up when you have a valid point to make. When I attend well-run meetings, they can often make my day because of the productivity and feeling of accomplishment. Too many times we go to meetings and even wonder why we are there. Do your part whether you're running the meeting or participating in it to make it valuable for all by adding value when you can.

As a leader, start off your meetings with a quick check-in with everyone before formally starting the meeting. Morag does what she calls "ripples and grins"—what have you experienced since the last meeting that caused you frustration or joy? What's something you've heard or experienced that brought a smile to your face? Sharing those can make people smile, open up, and set the tone for a more productive and participative meeting. This icebreaker doesn't have to be long—one to two minutes per person usually works; some will use less. Then share and stick to the agenda. You've provided ways to transition to a productive discussion and meeting while getting everyone warmed up to be active and participative.

You can raise your presence and make someone's day simply by being an involved meeting participant. Paying attention and offering input at the appropriate times is seen as valuable and builds trust. If you can get to meetings a little early and chat, you'll find the same scenario online as if you physically got to an in-person meeting a little early—a chance to talk about other business needs or mutual interests. I plan my meetings to start five to ten minutes early to allow for this connection time. An online chat with one another before a meeting is a great way to touch base and see how each other is doing and provides insight to make someone's day.

I've walked away from many meetings with feelings of joy and success when those meetings were done well and managed time well. It feels good to work with others who put out the effort and care about achieving our goal. This can also lead to higher performance, the hallmark of a high-performing team. When I have managed or participated on teams like this, it has led to some great accomplishments, including winning outstanding volunteer awards, meeting some of my closest friends, and of course hitting our goal in stellar fashion.

As a volunteer leader in ATD, I am always on the lookout for prospective volunteer leaders to mentor, matching them with both their interests and where I believe they can succeed. Many followed me up the leadership ladder and later told me it was my support and encouragement that got them there and made their day. Whenever I hear that, it feels great and makes my day. Letting me know that my support and advocacy inspired them to get involved as a leader is personally rewarding to hear. And how did I identify them? They showed up and stood out!

REACHING OUT AND BEING THERE

Curtis Martin is a Hall of Fame NFL football player. But he may not have gotten there if he wasn't noticed and if he didn't follow up and stand out. When Curtis was a junior at college, a scout showed up from the Senior Bowl. He gave Curtis his card and said, "I want to see you at the Senior Bowl next year no matter what." Curtis knew that conversation was his ticket to the NFL. The first game of his senior year, Curtis tore his ankle and couldn't play all year. Dejected, he remembered he had the card of this scout. Toward the end of the season, he called him, and immediately the scout said he was so sorry that Curtis tore his ankle and couldn't play this year. By then, though, the ankle had healed. So before he could hang up, Curtis said to the scout, "Remember you said to me you want to see me play at the Senior Bowl no matter what? I know I didn't play this year, but I want to play at the Senior Bowl. What can you do?" The scout thought for a minute and said to him, "If I can get you there, I can't guarantee that you'll play." Curtis said, "Fine, just get me there."

Curtis did get there with all the top seniors, but he was put low on the depth chart as a last-string fullback because he was injured all year. His preferred position was a running back, not a big fullback. But Curtis had heart and was going to take any opportunity he was given. He played with abandon at the position, blocking players far larger than he was, moving up the depth charts, and making an impression on the NFL scouts in attendance. They thought if he had this much passion at this unnatural spot, they could only imagine how good he would be in his true position. Curtis got drafted into the NFL and had a Hall of Fame career. Because he fought to show up and stand out, and when he did, he made the most of it and made his day and career.

Karolus had a party for his seventy-fifth birthday. Friends from different walks of his life showed up to celebrate him, and being an actor, author, coach, teacher, and consultant, his interests, abilities, and friendships spanned quite a range of people. Toward the end of the evening, Karolus thanked us all for coming. Spontaneously, before he could say goodbye, several friends stood up to toast him and acknowledge the contributions he made to their lives. Other people did the same. The stories and tributes were very touching and kept on coming. Karolus was extremely moved by the tributes from people he felt closest to and was delighted this impromptu acknowledgement happened. We all need to hear that now when we're alive and can appreciate it, not when we're gone. Each of us has many facets of our lives that others may not know about besides work—hobbies, long-term friends, activities, and causes we care about and may work on. People had no idea of all of the activities, projects, and work that Karolus did and the impact he had. His birthday party turned out to be a beautiful celebration of how he stood out throughout his life, and this reflection about it from others indeed made his day.

Think about doing that at the next milestone birthday of your spouse, sibling, friend, or colleague and make their day now when they can hear it and appreciate it by showing up and sharing. Let them know how they stand out to you!

My grandmother was a friend to all. People would see her walking on the street and stop to talk to her. She made time for everyone, especially those in her apartment building with her patience, warm glance, and open ears. When my sister and I visited her, her neighbors always wanted to see us and give us little gifts as a thank-you to her for being there for them. Little did I know that she was also setting me up for a lifetime of listening, caring about others, being friendly to all, and making someone's day.

SUPPORT PEOPLE AND STAFF ARE FAR MORE THAN THAT

How do you treat the people who support you and your work? Are they "invisible" because of their roles? Do you greet them with the same smile and hello as you would anyone at your level or above? Be friendly to everyone and let others see you show up and care about them. Maybe you'll get a chance to have some remarkable experiences as a result, just like my dad did in the following story.

My dad always showed up for his staff and workers. He made friends with everyone and always brought a smile, a ready ear, and a kind word to all. Among them was the nighttime custodian in his office. Joe was from Italy and taught my dad some Italian phrases when they took time to chat while Joe was cleaning the offices. Joe had a dream to open up a restaurant. Dad encouraged him and helped him to realize that dream. And guess who was one of the first patrons at Joe's restaurant? Yes, our family. But the restaurant business is tough; Joe missed his country and extended family and decided to move his family back to Italy, near Rome. A year later, my parents took us on our first trip to Europe, including three days in Rome. Dad had written Joe ahead of time, who insisted we go to his house for dinner. Joe picked us up when we arrived at our hotel in Rome and we headed to the countryside, which was actually near the Pope's summer home. After some pleasantries with his family and a house tour, we sat down for dinner. The meal started with delicious homemade pasta. As a young teenager, this was heaven, and when I was asked if I wanted seconds, who could say no? Little did I know that pasta was just the starter in a real Italian meal. I believe we had five or six courses. It was one of the most memorable meals I've ever had.

This unforgettable experience came about because my dad cared enough to talk with Joe and make his day when he was cleaning his office. My dad made friends everywhere. As a result of his friendships, we had other special outings as guests of his customers and colleagues that included viewing the Milwaukee Circus parade from an office balcony and spending the day on a boat on Lake Ontario. My dad showed up for them, and they showed up for him and his family.

HELPING THE CHILDREN IN YOUR LIFE

I think about my son, Jordan, in his first year at Boy Scout summer camp, which was his first overnight camp. Like many first-year campers, Jordan was feeling overwhelmed and out of place. I knew this because I was his Scoutmaster. One day we went to go mountain biking, and it was frustrating for Jordan to find the right bike because most were bigger and pretty banged up at that. He got so frustrated with trying to find a bike that worked well that he gave up. The camp ranger saw him, headed over, and bought him a soda and sat down to talk to him. I had tears in my eyes as I saw Jordan take a deep breath and feel better as the recipient of this small act of kindness and getting some extra attention. Thank you, Trent, for showing up in a way that did so much for my son and making the day for so many sons and daughters at camp.

Who has helped your son or daughter, niece or nephew, or sibling with a small act of kindness like that? What did they do that made a difference? It can be as simple as a conversation, giving them confidence, offering advice or even a summer job. Make Someone's Day moments don't need to be large. They can be nonverbal like listening, small like giving them a sweet treat, helpful like assisting them with finding a job. This can also occur online through praise, a referral, or a recommendation. The one thing they all have in common to make someone's day is that they happen when it's most needed and valued.

Friends can sometimes surprise you the most, as Neville shares. "Someone made my day last week by simply doing something for me because it was a nice thing to do. I'm a trustee for a young people's sports charity, and they made a donation. We discussed the initiative whilst playing for an over-sixty rugby team, and they went out of their way to take the details of the charity into their sports club and asked their committee to promote it to their members. This was going beyond the natural response of either donating or not. Having decided to donate financially, they asked for more detail on the work being done. It's aim is to encourage access and participation for those young people either disadvantaged or disabled, or for young women in rugby. They took the inclusivity and well-being message wider. Beyond financial support, they brought people together to open up facilities. As a result, they will positively impact the lives, energy, enjoyment, and well-being of young people. A fabulous example of the older generation putting back in for those in the younger generation in need of help to access the sport and make someone's day including mine with their actions!"

WHAT YOU WEAR CAN MAKE SOMEONE'S DAY

Sometimes people will say, "You made my day," and you don't even know why. How about showing up wearing the right t-shirt or cap? Do you like t-shirts with messages or logos on them? T-shirts, caps, and masks during the pandemic say something about the person wearing it. You usually wear one for a place, team, or cause you care about. I was wearing a Chicago Cubs t-shirt sponsored by a casual restaurant chain in Chicago called Portillo's while on my way to the exercise room of a hotel I was staying at in St. Louis. The front desk receptionist looked up at me and immediately said, "You made my day!" This was on the weekend of a Cubs-Cardinals series in St. Louis, not a time or place you get the warmest reactions wearing a rival Cubs shirt. Was she a Cubs fan? No, but she was from Chicago and a big fan of Portillo's, the sponsor of the shirt, and seeing her favorite restaurant on the shirt excited her. That's all I did, evidently wear the right t-shirt. And her memories flooded back to her. How simple is that to do? (Now you just have to figure out what's the right shirt to wear!)

Remember the V in the VIP Model is View/Observe? When someone wears a shirt, cap, hat, or jacket with a favorite sports team or activity, that gives you a clue as to what they care about. Use that information to help make their day when the situation is right.

SUPPORT DURING JOB HUNTING

Supporting others who are networking and job hunting get a new lead or connection can seriously make their day. These can be some of the most frustrating and challenging times in life as you try and find a job that fits your talents, provides for growth, and you can enjoy and contribute to successfully. When searching for a new job, you're starting at the bottom of the Maslow hierarchy of needs, where safety, security, and family needs are most pressing. Too often the process feels like you're in a tunnel and don't know how long it is and when the end will be in sight. During these times of aggravation, angst, and doubt, we can never have enough people helping to make our day to keep our spirits up. A referral, suggestion, or motivation and support can help make all the difference.

A great analogy is selling a house or car. You work hard to stage it properly so it gets a buyer's attention and you can get the best offer. Same goes for job hunting. You put on your best professional outfit, practice what you will say, and show your most positive side when you're networking and interviewing. That way you're staging yourself. Lindsey Pollak, in her book *Recalculating*, talks about job hunting is like using a GPS—you're constantly recalculating to find your best path and direction.

If you're the one job hunting, always be aware of your actions. You need to both show up and show up in the right way. Remember staging the house? You are staging yourself every time you go out or online for an interview or networking. A friend of mine from Southwest Airlines tells the story of someone who interviewed for a job with the airline, which is known for their customer attention. The interviewee was flying to Southwest's Dallas headquarters for their final interview. For some reason, they were rude to the first person they met at the gate in their home city. Word traveled quickly. By the time they got to Dallas, they were asked to turn around and were immediately flown back home. Their behavior at their home gate was not a fit with Southwest's customer-focused culture. Always be on your best behavior and know you are always on stage when you're job hunting. Remember to make someone's day who may be helping you while you travel to your interview. These positive stories will travel just as fast as negative ones do and can make the difference between getting the job or not.

SHOWING UP FOR SOMEONE WHEN THEY'VE LOST A LOVED ONE

There's no greater time of need for showing up than when someone dies. One of the most important acts of loving kindness you can do for others is showing up to support friends and family at a funeral, a wake, a shiva, or a period of mourning. Showing up for others can mean so much to the people you care about when they are experiencing the loss of someone close. In this example, I'm sure no one would say, "You made my day," by your being there, but it is greatly appreciated in that same light. Whether you can share a story, provide a joke to lighten the mood, or just listen, mourners truly appreciate your sympathies and will always remember that you made the effort to be there and comfort them.

Speaking of funerals, I find it remarkable how much we can learn about people from eulogies, even when we thought we knew someone well. Have you learned something surprising or remarkable about someone you thought you knew well? We need to hear those stories before they are no longer with us. The person themselves needs to hear how much we appreciate them, much like was done for Karolus mentioned earlier.

SHOWING UP FOR SOMEONE ILL

Visiting family, friends, and close colleagues when they are ill is also a way to make their day. The act of visiting or calling can make a world of difference when trying to recover from an illness or operation. Sharing a story, memory, or joke is most appreciated and often is a "you made my day" moment. They appreciate the visit and the distraction from thinking about how they feel or being poked and prodded. Here's some research to show the importance of this action.

A short visit is as meaningful as a long one and sometimes can make someone's day in more ways than you imagine. Angela Epstein of *The Daily Mail* explains: "Though it might seem like a chore to you, visiting a sick friend or relative in the hospital really could make a difference to their health. Recent research has shown it's what your visit does to their brain that helps. A close relationship with a friend, partner, or relative has been found to halve the risk of heart patients having another cardiac arrest—while a lack of a close confidant puts sufferers at a greater risk of having further heart attacks. Positive emotions have also been shown to increase a person's resistance to and overcoming illness." Scientists have discovered why, as described back in chapter three. Epstein continues, "Mirror neurons are activated when we experience an emotion. More crucially, they also fire off when we watch others experience feelings we can identify with, leading us to mimic these sentiments and become infected by the mood. During and after a visit from a loving and cheerful friend or relation, mirror neurons will stir similar positive feelings in the brain of the patient, lifting their spirits and making them feel better." The neuroscience behind making someone's day keeps showing up—as long as you keep showing up.

My wife Laurie had a chance to show up for her father. Ed Frank was a journalist and Public Affairs professional who gave a hand to anyone who needed it. He was constantly driving people to medical appointments over an hour away. Ed recently had an illness scare himself that hospitalized him. When Laurie visited him, he asked her to write down the highlights of his life—how he made decisions on where to go to school, what to study, where to work, etc. She teased him and said, "What about writing about your kids?" and he said, "You know all that stuff!" As hard as it was for her to be writing this down, some of the insights she gained about her father were great to hear and things she didn't know. Her dad was happy that he was able to do this with her, and her spending extra time with him made his day. Laurie showed up and was there for him. That's just what he needed.

SHOWING UP AT WORK

Many companies have celebrations for people on their work anniversaries. When the numbers get larger (double digits), they may hold a special celebration that is open to others in the company, like a cake and coffee reception. Showing up to those does three things: 1) it shows respect for the person being honored, 2) it gives you a chance to mingle with others in the office who you may not get a chance to talk to or see regularly, and 3) it keeps you in the know of what's going on. It also can make someone's day by seeing you there to recognize them.

When showing up, it's also important to show up positively. That can make so much difference. Amy Finlay, co-founder of Edinburgh IFA, says, "Having a positive attitude in the workplace won't necessarily make you better at your job, but it will improve the way people view you as a person, so they may be more inclined to help you succeed and cheer you on. One of the main reasons for having a positive attitude in the workplace is because it can rub off on everyone else. Exuding positivity can be infectious and, over time, can influence your coworkers."

Deborah Sweeney, CEO of MyCorporation, talks about other ways of showing up at work that make a difference. "You can show a positive attitude through the words you use," Sweeney says. "Become a 'yes' person and try new things to see how you do. Give your time and ask coworkers how you can help them out if you have a free moment. Volunteer to take the lead on new assignments. Be kind to everyone and be genuine—don't gossip or spread rumors." Isn't this giving others the VIP treatment—saying yes, volunteering, and helping them out? These are all ways you can show up at work and make someone's day.

SHOWING UP FOR STRANGERS IN NEED

When Laurie and I got married, we decided that we wanted to spend part of "our weekend" showing up for others and make someone's day. We decided we would take our dog Spencer and visit patients and residents of a senior living and rehab facility. Spencer was my first dog, and we thought he was so friendly and cute that others would enjoy just seeing and petting him. That was definitely the case. The joy residents and patients had by our visit and seeing Spencer made their day. It brought gladness to our hearts to lift others up on our special weekend when we were being celebrated. We showed up to others we didn't even know.

How can doing laundry for someone make someone's day? In the foreword to the book, Marshall Goldsmith talked about his experience with Frances Hesselbein surprising him by doing his laundry when she was CEO of GSUSA. Here's another. Fiona was walking out of a meeting at a local hotel in DC and overheard a family saying, "What are we going to do?" Their young infant son just threw up several times, and they were out of clean clothes. They were from Italy, visiting the US, and not sure how they would get clean clothes as he had gone through all the clothes they brought with them. Fiona said to them, "Give me your laundry and I'll do it for you." The couple looked at her, bewildered. She said, "Trust me, I can do it easily and have it back to you the next day," and she did. They didn't know how to repay her for her kindness, and she simply said, "Help someone out when they're visiting Italy." Did she make their day and trip? Indeed.

VOLUNTEER

The Business Times in 2012 quantified and discussed the value of volunteering. "People volunteer for an endless variety of reasons: gain experience, acquire new skills, meet new people, or expand their network of contacts as a way to get a new job or start a career. Others just want to give back to their community, help a friend, or promote a worthwhile activity." And we know why it makes them feel good—because often they are making someone's day when they volunteer. They're helping out others, working with like-minded people, and making a difference. Do you volunteer? How do you show up when you do? Whenever and wherever you can in life, show up, be there, be counted, and make someone's day better.

PUTTING INTO PRACTICE

Sometimes the hardest thing to do is to show up. There are so many reasons not to, including you've had a long day, you're tired, you may not know the people, you don't feel like it, the weather is bad, or the traffic is worse. When you can cut through these excuses and do show up, be sure to stand out through your words, actions, enthusiasm, and support. You never know who's watching and how it can help.

Who's been a mentor, a role model, or a concerned friend who showed up for you in your life? Do they know how they've helped you? Contact them right away to say thanks. What's one thing you can do to show up and stand out? Make plans to do that, and if you can, do so regularly.

Many of the actions discussed so far can often be easier for extroverts. Introverts can also participate and make someone's day. Chapter six discusses how.

CHAPTER 6

. . . .

MAKE SOMEONE'S DAY
FOR INTROVERTS

"The best way to find yourself is to lose yourself in the service of others."
—Mahatma Gandhi

AS I'VE SAID OR intimated through the book so far, I am an extrovert, meaning I get energy from connecting and communicating with others. However, many people aren't. Make Someone's Day is for everyone— extrovert and introvert alike. In this chapter, learn ways you can make someone's day and put Make Someone's Day to use without extra or unnecessary interaction. Because we all benefit when we make someone's day.

According to the website Lifehack, "Introverts are everywhere (one out of every two or three people you know). And they are like icebergs. What you see on the surface is only a small percentage of their entire selves. It's just that they don't usually help people to see the rest of them or the strengths they bring to the work environment. If you work with an introverted person, you're going to have to look for the substance underneath to fully appreciate them and their incredibly valuable input at work. Keep in mind that introversion seems to increase with intelligence so that more than seventy-five percent of people with an IQ above 160 are introverted." That's powerful to know because introverts by their nature wouldn't be expounding on that.

FIVE CHARACTERISTICS OF INTROVERTS

An article on Lifehack by David K. William goes into greater detail on what introverts do at work that helps them succeed. Let me share a few of those.

1) **Introverts think through an issue before they speak.** Joe McHugh, vice president of executive services for the Edina, Minnesota, office of Right Management Consultants, explains: "Colleagues and bosses need to realize that introverts often don't know what they think immediately, and that they need time to think things through before coming to a conclusion. It's critical that you circle back to introverts after they've had some time to consider things." This thoughtful reflection can lead to great insights and ideas. Make sure you get everyone's input and give people information in advance so when you meet, everyone will have had a chance to think through the issues you're discussing.

2) **Introverts like getting to the point.** Sophia Dembling, author of *The Introvert's Way: Living a Quiet Life in a Noisy World*, explains, "It ultimately comes down to how a person receives (or doesn't receive) energy from his or her surroundings. Introverts are great listeners; we're good at drawing people out; and we're often a lot more comfortable listening than talking." Those are strengths that all teams need—good listeners, people who seek to understand and use questions to better understand. They prefer getting to the point over what may seem like endless small talk. In meetings and conversations, give people an agenda and get to the point.

3) **Introverts support those they lead.** David William writes, "The reason introverts do so well in leadership positions is because they thrive by listening carefully, even to suggestions from below. It is

second nature for introverted bosses to listen, appreciate and validate great ideas, and highly unlikely for them to treat those they lead condescendingly." Take Doug Conant, an introvert and former CEO of Campbell's Soup. Doug has been celebrated for writing more than thirty thousand personalized thank-you notes to his employees. It's hard to imagine an extrovert taking the time to do that. Attention to all while supporting the people we lead is a great characteristic to have. You'll learn more about Doug later.

4) **Introverts have an attitude of observance, reflection, and caution.** *Forbes* contributing author Christina Park, an introvert, writes, "Introverts like to prepare for meetings and presentations, rather than 'winging it.' This offers several benefits. First, you show that you really care about your work and are invested in the outcome. Second, you can collect facts in advance and gather your ideas in an organized fashion. Finally, preparation allows you to identify potential problems and propose solutions (or spark discussion around the issue)." There's a lot to be said for everyone providing thoughtful preparations and preparing for meetings.

5) **Introverts like to work individually and don't need to have people around them.** Reports David William, "Just because introverts are self-reflective and dislike being interrupted at work doesn't mean they hate people. Far from it; they just tend to do their best work on their own, prefer a few good friends over many acquaintances, and need to be given air time as they typically will not demand it. Once you give them that and understand they are more reserved, you can establish a deep and fulfilling personal and professional relationship with them." As an extrovert, I want to make friends with everyone. To me, the more the merrier, but then I'm often embarrassed if I don't remember why we connected or how we met in the first place. Introverts choose a careful few so they are much easier to remember and are quieter on teams because they're thinking.

As you see from the above five characteristics, the value introverts bring to the workplace is substantial. Introverts may have a harder time making someone's day for someone they don't know and may be more comfortable doing so just for colleagues that they know well or supporting you in your efforts to make someone's day. I'm an assessor for the Certificate Accreditation Program of the ANSI National Accreditation Board (ANAB). When I am teamed up with someone who is more introverted, they can bring up points I may have missed. We complement each other and make a good team. And by doing a thorough assessment for our client, that makes our client's day.

THE USE OF SOCIAL MEDIA AND THE LIKE BUTTON

What about the use of social media if you're more introverted or don't like having a conversation with a stranger? Journalist Ted Koppel had a chance to interview Justin Rosenstien, co-inventor of the "Like" button on Facebook, on *CBS Sunday Morning*, on April 1, 2018.

Ted Koppel inquired about what was going through Justin's mind when he created the like button when he interviewed him on *Sunday Morning*. Justin said, "I wanted to make something really easy—one click—for people to share little bits of positivity and affirmation in the world." How simple to do. The like button on Facebook and other social media provides a simple way to acknowledge someone and their thoughts, ideas, or images they are sharing. How often do you do that? Especially when I'm rushed, I use the like button a lot to let people know I saw and liked their post.

Much like a smile, being liked more often has similar psychological effects, according to the blog *Start Digital*. "We get a dopamine (and other neurochemical) rush when our post gets attention and likes or every time we get thumbs up or an emoji. And we keep getting them as people continue to like our post, to the point that it becomes a feeding loop—the more people like our post, the more we get a dopamine rush. This loop causes us to seek it even more (and to look for the thumbs-up and likes)."

According to a study about online posts published in the *Association for Psychological Science Journal* in 2016, "The impact on our brain is like eating chocolate or winning at the casino. When teenagers see people liking their photos and posts, it becomes a very positive form of engagement." If enough people do that, the feeling can be similar to hearing, "You made my day." Think about how you feel when people like your post or comment. It feels good to get that affirmation and to know that our messages are connecting with others.

What's remarkable on social media is the people who follow you and look forward to your posts that you don't even know about. During the pandemic, my wife Laurie started baking challah bread every Friday, and I posted a picture of it each week. She'd come up with many variations from allspice to garlic and rosemary to sour dough and even a red, white, and blue twist for July 4th. What I didn't know was that one of the people who always looked forward to the photo and post was my brother-in-law Phil. When he called us one day, he asked, "Can you tell me in advance what kind of challah you are baking today?" Sounds silly, but that made my day because it confirmed people were following my posts even if they didn't comment.

I try to acknowledge birthdays and appreciate the way social media reminds us. Often a day or two later, the person whose birthday it is writes how delighted they are with their birthday wishes and how good it made them feel. Have you experienced that, too? One year, I took time on my birthday to read many of the comments people posted, and they made my day. Maybe not the best way to spend my birthday, but it was rewarding to read and see comments from friends and family. And even for those who just "liked" my birthday, it brought a smile to me when I saw the list of people who took a little effort to "like" my birthday. What about you—do you read the comments from others about your posts, pictures, birthday, and special occasions? Introverted or extroverted, how does that make you feel?

Larry Rosen writes in *Psychology Today* that he was mentoring a high school student who celebrated his seventeenth birthday. He wished him a belated congratulations a couple of days later and asked how his birthday was. Michael grabbed his smartphone and said, "Did you see that I got

129 likes, Dr. Rosen? That's the most ever—wow!" What a powerful impact the simple like button can have.

Kate has done a great job organizing our high school reunions and posting everyone's birthday each day in our reunion group on Facebook. I can send anyone from my class a note wishing them well on their birthday thanks to the daily posting reminder from Kate. As a way of connecting our large high school graduating class, she has done a great job of pulling us together this way.

Gene Siskel and Roger Ebert made the thumbs-up a popular statement of approval in their movie reviews. Whether done on social media or live, a thumbs-up provides a feeling of approval and agreement. We smile when we get a thumbs-up and know we're on track. It's an affirmation that leads to the feeling of "I'm good, I'm on track" and can even lead to "you made my day" feelings. What's fascinating is that people can get similar neurological benefits from doing so.

When I co-facilitate training programs with a colleague, a thumbs-up from my partner lets me know I'm on track, people are paying attention, and the session is going well. That's very helpful to know when you're focused on teaching and managing discussion and exercises. It's even more helpful to know when teaching online. Having someone who can manage the chat while I'm teaching and ensure that questions are all addressed is invaluable.

ADDING COMMENTS

What's even more powerful than liking a photo or post is when you add a comment. Facebook is one of the most studied and analyzed social media platforms because of its huge number of users, 2.85 billion as of the end of the first half of 2021, and of that number, 1.88 billion visit on a daily basis. I'm sure by the time you're reading this chapter that the number is over three billion users. Facebook may be the best way to contact everyone on the planet if there was a global emergency.

There are lots of analytics and research that go into understanding the dynamics of Facebook. Let's examine the neurological impact of Facebook, the part that makes someone's day. A recent study discovered that there is a strong connection between Facebook and the nucleus accumbens region of the brain, which processes our feelings of being rewarded. Positive feedback on Facebook lights up this part of our brain. The more we interact with Facebook users (and I'll expand that to social media users), the greater reward we receive.

Something interesting about receiving comments is how our brain reacts to comments as compared to likes. Dr. Moira Burke, a research scientist at Facebook, is studying 1,200 Facebook users in an ongoing experiment. She found that personal messages are more satisfying to receivers than the one-click communication of likes. She calls them "composed communication," which she describes further. "In an era where it's all too easy for people to stay isolated and alone, composed communication helps people feel less alone. Posts with just a like experienced no change in loneliness. Even better than sending a private Facebook message is the semi-public conversation, the kind of back-and-forth in which you half ignore the other people who may be listening in, because this too helps decrease loneliness in people."

The US Surgeon General for the Obama and Biden administrations, Vice Admiral Dr. Vivek Murthy, wrote the book *Together: The Healing Power of Human Connection in A Sometimes Lonely World*. He wrote, "At the center of our loneliness is our innate desire to connect. We have evolved as a species to participate in community, to forge lasting bonds with others, to help one another, and to share life experiences. We are simply better together." Connecting with others online can help ease loneliness by showing that we are not alone. Especially in times when we are quarantined or semi-quarantined, this is so important. As described more in chapter ten, mental health and suicide rates have increased dramatically during the time of the pandemic and greater isolation.

A report in *Scientific American* of March 2014 by Krystal D'Costa reported, "Introverts aren't going to be the friends who Like everything. These are the people you're surprised to hear from. They'll peruse their feed and respond at length to the items that resonate most strongly with them. The rest of the time, they're absorbing information about others—reading updates, viewing photos, and thinking about the shared content and comments without responding publicly. This information doesn't necessarily go to waste; it can be leveraged in subsequent face-to-face interactions. While there's a chance that highly introverted individuals may find that having lots of personal information about another person is overwhelming especially in a one-to-one interaction offline, others may be able to use this information to ease their off-line interactions. It provides a basis from which they can navigate social encounters because it gives them something to know; it helps foster a connection so it reduces the stress in establishing a relationship."

Communicating online allows for a degree of distance that can be helpful for introverts and allows time for thoughtful responses that can make someone's day, rather than immediate knee-jerk responses. Email allows you a chance to read, reflect, and respond when you are ready. Instant messaging is not quite the same. Something about IM leads to a sense of urgency to respond at that instant. Both email and IM allow you to remain more private because you're dealing with others online and not face-to-face, providing a degree of distance that introverts prefer.

WEBSITES THAT ENCOURAGE MAKING SOMEONE'S DAY

There are so many ways to connect and make someone's day online, such as Caring Bridge. For people with serious illnesses, it's a great way for families to communicate with friends and followers that is far less taxing than sending regular email blasts or returning hundreds of phone calls and messages. Caring Bridge is exactly that—a bridge to someone you care about who has suffered an accident or illness. With the family posting even the little steps toward improvement, friends and relatives can learn about the progress and respond as desired to make someone's day through words of encouragement, care, friendship, and support to both the patient and their family.

Responding online isn't just for introverts. Many of us love to do something that helps others and makes their day but often aren't sure how to do so online. *Millennial Magazine* published "20 Websites That Can Help You Make a Difference." Here are just a few of the many places and causes recommended at this time that can be supported online and make someone's day through your actions. Be careful typing them in your browser and use the correct ending—.com, .org, etc.

1) **Change.org.** "The World's Platform for Change" lets users learn more about causes that are happening locally as well as around the globe. For example, users sign petitions to show support for people who are being harmed. This is more of a make someone's collective day, but the boomerang effect of doing something helpful can still apply.

2) **Kiva.org.** Kiva lets you make a difference by making loans for people in need, and it's tagline is "Loans that change lives." Many of the items for which money is being requested are very modest, like detergent for starting a laundry, soft drinks for a business in Kenya, or fertilizer and manure for a struggling farmer. Loans can be for as little as twenty-five dollars. You are definitely making someone's day through this critical loan lifeline for people in need or wanting to start a business that can sustain them. You choose both where the money goes and how much. One hundred percent goes to the cause you are funding.

3) **Care2.com.** Founded in 1998, this website combines topics like healthy living, environmental sustainability, and humane animal treatment and empowers people to get involved on a global level. Their tagline is "Care2 gives you the tools to make the impossible possible." You may not feel or hear the words, "You made my day," but you may get the boomerang effect if you become supportive of their work as they have many digital badges you can earn from helping.

4) **DoSomething.org.** Geared toward young people and called "the youth-led movement for good," this website offers a database

of opportunities that prove how it's possible to get involved with something that matters even if you only have a few minutes of spare time. And it's very action-oriented. What a cool way to make someone's day and do it in a way that fits your schedule and time demands.

5) **DonorsChoose.org.** Founded by a high school teacher in the Bronx and with Oprah Winfrey liking this, it's gotten very popular. Their slogan is "wherever learning happens, you can make a difference." Donations go to teachers who need supplies for their classrooms and post specific requests. It's nice to choose where and what your support goes to, and you can feel like you've made someone's day by getting school supplies to where they are most needed.

6) **Bekindr.com.** Bekindr is a movement to bring more kindness to the world. Founded by author and psychiatrist Eva Ritvo, MD, and others, this free website provides stories, blogs, and resources around acts of kindness.

These websites and more provide a good start for making someone's day in a way that's easy for introverts or anyone who would prefer to do so online and/or anonymously. And it only takes a little time or a little money. You don't hear the words "you made my day" said, but in fact that is exactly what others experience from your support.

PUTTING INTO PRACTICE

Make Someone's Day is for everyone. Remember to acknowledge, invite, and incorporate the insights of introverts in your work. You don't necessarily have to hear the words "you made my day" to have a similar experience online. Through likes and comments, you can sense the same thing. And for those who lean toward being introverted, it allows you to participate in making someone's day in your own way, whether online or with your closest colleagues and friends.

Are you an introvert or an extrovert? Introvertdear.com has a free profile you can complete to understand your preferences, realizing that there are no pure extroverts or introverts. Find out where your tendencies lie and reach out to someone with an opposite inclination to work on a project together. It can be a big or small project for work or as a volunteer. Determine who will lead the project and what you will each be responsible for. Keep notes of how you work together and what you learn from the other person's style as a result.

Chapter seven describes what it's like to work on a larger project or do things in a much bigger but not necessarily more difficult way, to make someone's day and even their life.

CHAPTER 7

....

GOING ALL IN

"There is no exercise better for the heart than reaching down and lifting people up." —John Holmes

GOING ALL IN MEANS doing something big. It can be hard or strenuous, or it may be easy for you but hard for others to do. It can involve more planning, tasks, and time. This may lead to changing some thinking, shifting a perception, or even saving a life.

An example of someone making my day in a big way happened when I was asked what's new at a board alumni dinner. A client and I had recently won an Excellence in Practice award from an international educational association, EFMD. The graduate school where I worked had no budget for me to attend the conference in Germany and receive the award. I was disappointed but still glad to have won this award, one in only five in the world. I happened to mention this informally at a board alumni dinner of my professional association a few weeks later. A past president of the association and I were sitting next to each other, and he said to me, "My foundation looks for people like you that we can help. You have your funding. Just write it up and go make arrangements to receive your award." I was speechless. It was an amazing offer of generosity from

Martin—someone I had met and chatted with the last few years at this annual dinner. I am forever grateful that I mentioned something to him that day about winning this award. You never know when someone is in a position to make your day in a big way!

COMPANIES DO TOO

Companies can do this too—big for you, small for them. Nordstrom's is famous for its customer service. In the past, they've even taken back merchandise they didn't sell, such as snow tires! (They don't do this anymore.) Dan was at a conference in San Diego and wandered over to Nordstrom's in the evening the night before the end of the conference. Nordstrom's was having their twice-yearly men's sale, and he bought two suits. The only problem was he was leaving at noon the next day to get back to the East Coast. "No problem," the salesclerk said. "Have your taxi swing by, and we'll have your suits altered and ready to pick up." Dan was running late at the conference and didn't have time to stop by Nordstrom's on his way to the airport. The next day, by overnight delivery, Dan received his two suits, with two free silk ties. The clerk was so sorry he couldn't stop by and wanted to be sure he was happy with his purchase. Who knows how many suits Dan will buy in his lifetime, but where do you think he's going to get them? Nordstrom's created a customer for life.

Often unexpected problems pop up while traveling. When these surprise delays happen, you can easily become anxious and frustrated. That's where Belle Tires in Michigan City, Indiana, came in, and in a big way for us. We were driving to pick up my father-in-law in Michigan City, and the "check tire" light went on. Our car dashboard showed the tire pressure was going down and quickly! Fortunately, we were close to the exit, got off, and immediately looked for a tire store. Belle Tires was fairly new to Michigan City and not far from the exit. We pulled in as the tire pressure was inching toward single digits and told the manager about the check-tire light. Could he see what might be wrong with the tires? No problem, he just needed about thirty minutes. We worried that we might have to get new tires and be substantially delayed on our trip or end up having to buy four new tires, which was not in our budget and not what we needed. We just wanted to solve the problem and get on our way and hopefully it not cost a fortune in the process. They pulled the car into the bay while we nervously awaited the outcome. We learned that not one but two tires on one side of the car had something in them. Perhaps we drove over some objects that we didn't see? After thirty minutes, the manager said the tires were repaired. Repaired? That was great news! We asked him how much it would be, expecting that whatever they charged would be fine—they were quick and saved us from having to buy new tires, which could have easily happened. After all, his business was selling tires. What do you think he said? Free. "This is just part of our service," the manager said. Not only did he fix the tires, he didn't charge us. Remarkable. He said we should come back when we needed new tires. Immediately, my stepdaughter Annie posted on Instagram and Facebook what a remarkable experience we had. My father-in-law shared the story with others in his wide network around town. My wish is that Belle Tires does a lot of business, because they surely made our day—and got us safely back on the road.

In my work developing leadership programs, I created a service-learning process where participants would practice their newly learned skills while at the same time helping community organizations. Are you learning financial skills? Put it to practice while volunteering for a nonprofit on the finance committee. Want to gain experience using new marketing or computer skills? Many nonprofits need your help! Want to practice one-on-one mentoring, coaching, or counseling? There are many ways to do this, and students in grade school through college need your time and skill. It gives leaders increased confidence in the skill while helping many worthy organizations. Here are just a few examples.

Doug was a quality manager at a manufacturing plant and wanted to improve his one-on-one communication, mentoring, and coaching skills. He volunteered to mentor six at-risk high school seniors, at risk of not graduating. Nine months later at the end of the leadership program and school year, he reported to the class that he failed. Really, what happened?

He said only five out of six graduated on time. The rest of us couldn't believe that—we thought he did exceptionally well and was overly hard on himself. Out of curiosity, I asked why didn't the sixth graduate? He said that her parents didn't see the value of her graduating high school! That didn't stop her—she got her GED later that summer. Imagine the impact Doug had on these six lives. Would you like to be mentored or coached by him? I would!

One creative purchasing agent developed what he called SHOP—Save Homeless Office Products. He figured many people had office supplies in their offices they didn't or couldn't use (e.g. printer ink that doesn't fit your new printer, etc.). People "donated" office products they weren't using and were able to choose items they did need at a SHOP fair. The result: over $30,000 was saved for the organization through this redistribution and fun was had by all. People got rid of things they didn't need and found things that they did need—making their day!

IN BIG WAYS FOR THE COMMUNITY

Father Gregory Boyle tries to make many people's day and provide reassurance for a group often ignored and discriminated against. In 1986, Father Greg became pastor of Dolores Mission Church, the poorest Catholic parish in Los Angeles with the largest public housing projects in the western US. At the time, this area also had the highest concentration of gang activity. Law enforcement used mass incarceration as their way to deal with the crime. Father Greg had a different perspective. He saw people in need of help and started Homeboy Industries in 1992, which has become the largest gang intervention, rehabilitation, and re-entry program in the world. Here's one success story from his effort. "Mario was a former gang member, tall and skinny, with more tattoos than anyone had ever seen over his entire body, including his shaved head. His eyelids were tattooed 'the end,' so that when he got shot, people would know he was gone. He even looked scary to other gang members. After he was released from jail, Mario began working for Homeboy as a sales clerk, and Father Greg asked him to speak at an event together with him. This former tough-as-nails gang member was scared to death of using a microphone and speaking to a crowd. But he did, sharing the story of his early gang life, prison, and how he's changed working at Homeboy. There wasn't a dry eye in the house. After he spoke, a woman in the audience asked him, 'I heard you have a son and a daughter. What do you tell them to be when they grow up?' He choked back a bit, nervously picked up the mic, and said, 'Not like me.' After hearing his story and seeing videos of him and how helpful and kind he has become from his work with Homeboy as a sales clerk, the questioner did not miss a beat and said, 'Why not? You are the kindest, most caring, and giving person I have met here. That's exactly what your kids should aspire to be.'" Whatever magic Father Greg is doing, he's making people's lives in a big way.

Father Corey is executive director of Viator House of Hospitality. VHH has been helping youth who reach the US seeking asylum. Sent by their families with whatever they could carry, these journeys started on every continent in the world and led literally thousands of miles to the US border. As they aged out of federal immigrant youth immigration programs and turned eighteen while waiting for their hearing, without a place to stay, they would have been put in jail awaiting their hearing. Instead, Viator House for men and Bethany House of Hospitality for women provide a group home, food, learning, and education so that when their cases are brought before a judge, they are well on their way to being a working and productive part of American society. Father Corey and the many volunteers at these homes truly make their days and their lives.

What about making someone's day for seniors with Alzheimer's or memory loss? Nancy is a high school friend who went on to a magnificent career as an opera star in Europe. She now teaches voice at Northwestern University and discovered something when she visited her mother. "I was visiting my mother in her memory care unit in Costa Mesa, California, and was saddened by how quickly her health declined. So I decided to try to get her to sing with me. I started playing the piano. The piano was never one of my strong suits—but I tried my hand at some Christmas carols. Mom slowly started singing along . . . notwithstanding my piano playing. After about fifteen minutes of playing, I turned to look at her, and she said, 'You know that's not very good.' I nearly cried. I was so happy. Mom was actually expressing a thought. And an honest one at that! We laughed, and I told her that I would choose easier pieces for the piano. We continued singing, and after another few songs, I looked at Mom—singing along with me—and once again she was able to talk and said, 'You're getting better.' I laughed with her and told her that if we improved enough, she and I could sing in the shopping malls at Christmas time and earn some money. She replied without missing a beat, 'Yeah, the Gustafson family singers.' It was at that moment that I knew what I had to do. I didn't want another day to pass where my mother and others like her sat in their rooms disconnected from the world around them, looking so terribly lost, depressed, and frightened. Music has the power to help people with memory loss connect to each other, the world around them, and to the joy of music. I would create a program that harnessed that power and aimed to improve the lives of people, like my mother, every day." Nancy started the Songs by Heart Foundation, which is now in dozens of communities across the US. By making her mom's day, Nancy learned how she could make the day of many other moms and dads in memory units with this vital work.

During the pandemic when my mom couldn't leave her apartment, we were most thankful she had her caregiver Clavel with her. Clavel was her constant companion and would find videos and concerts that she and Mom would enjoy together. I wanted to contribute, too, so every afternoon, I would pick some musicals or songs from the classic songbook and play them on tuba for my mom online. It was a real treat for me to keep up my playing and bring some smiles to Mom's face when I played some of her favorite songs. When she was in rehab for a few weeks after an accident when Illinois was starting to open up as the pandemic was diminishing, I even brought my tuba with me and played in her room. As she was leaving there, one of the nurses came up to me and asked if I was the tuba player. I was ready to be called out for not following some policy or disturbing others, but instead he said how many patients appreciated the music and couldn't believe a tuba could play that well. You know that made my day!

Making someone's day in a big way doesn't mean you have to create an organization or meet the needs of underserved populations of ex-cons. It can be much simpler, like me playing tuba on Zoom. What are your skills and talents? Do you have repair or building skills, shopping skills, music or art talent, teaching or tutoring skills, organizing skills? Do you like working with young people, adults, new employees, immigrants, or seniors? The need for your talent is huge in and outside of the workplace, and it can strengthen your own skills as you use them. Organizations need your help, from animal shelters to nursing homes to public parks and museums as tutors, docents, and volunteers. Organizations need you, like the Scouts and Girl Scouts, Habitat for Humanity, the Salvation Army at holiday time especially, and what is becoming a tradition in the US, a day of service on the Martin Luther King, Jr. holiday. These organizations and many more use volunteers to give back and make someone's day in a big way, by doing something planned and impactful.

PUTTING INTO PRACTICE

Going all in—making someone's day in a big way—may mean a bigger scope, more people, or just more planning and effort on your part.

Stop now and think about what you like to do and where you would like to volunteer. No experience necessary! As you continue reading this chapter, decide what resonates with you. We'll talk about it further at the end of the chapter.

MENTOR AND VOLUNTEER

Often help can come from a mentor, someone we admire or respect and want to learn from. We all need help or advice throughout our lives whatever level we are. Jennifer shares the story of how someone changed her life and career at the highest level. "One of my early discoveries of 2018 was that I was CEO-ready. I didn't realize this until, when doing a job search, one of my male colleagues told me I was ready. I've run my own consulting firm; I've been at the helm of corporate business units;

and I've engaged with countless impressive women executives. And yet, I hadn't envisioned the next logical step. As I contemplated the next phase in my career, I had several other male executives tell me I should just 'go run my own company' or 'take over as CEO of a venture in need of a strong leader.' They said this quickly as if it's a conclusion they drew long ago, but it was an awakening for me. I remember the exact moment that my dear friend and peer Christoffer made my day. He said, 'What are you waiting for? You are perfectly positioned for a CEO role at this time. If not now, when?' It was almost precisely at that moment I shifted away from my inner critic and self-doubt. That wake-up call allowed me to resist questioning my own readiness for the 'big job' when so many trusted men saw me in that role." Making someone's day does not need to be a monumental act. Christoffer made Jennifer's day by changing her perception of what she was meant to do in her career. Has anyone helped you or encouraged you during your career in such a way, opening doors either in reality or mentally for you to take on a greater challenge?

The small business development council (SBDC) provides volunteer business coaches to work with individuals and small businesses. Each provides the knowledge needed to help make someone's day. Fernando was so helpful to me as my SBDC coach that I sought him out specifically and met with him several times, each time providing me guidance and reassurance that I was on the right track. That made my day every time we met! SCORE does this, too. "SCORE's mission is to foster vibrant small business communities through mentoring and education. With the nation's largest network of volunteers and expert business mentors, SCORE has helped more than 11 million entrepreneurs since 1964." Art is a former marketing executive and SCORE volunteer who provided tremendous help with some marketing advice on this book. Thank you, Art and Fernando, for the wisdom and guidance you openly gave me and many others.

Many companies offer volunteer opportunities for employees, such as volunteering with United Way, Junior Achievement, company blood drives for blood banks, Toys for Tots, etc. Some organizations plan group volunteer outings to paint local schools, clean up city and neighborhood parks, etc. as a service to the community. When I worked for Waste Management, they celebrated Earth Day by cleaning up some of the major downtown Chicago parks. Many employees brought their kids and were provided with equipment, special t-shirts, and snacks. It made the day fun for everyone participating with all the good will and support and in turn cleaned up some of Chicago's largest city parks in the process. What a great way to show your kids the importance of volunteering and doing something good for the community.

Companies often encourage volunteering in non-profit organizations and expect to see their senior executives on various philanthropic boards. When leaders and executives put their hearts into this work, they are definitely making someone's day by helping many worthy organizations.

Aim High is a program where volunteers from sponsoring companies mentor inner-city youth from challenging neighborhoods, encouraging them to finish high school and get a college degree. "This ground-breaking student mentoring initiative's goal is to ensure that 100% of participating students graduate from high school, enter college, graduate from college, and gain the skills needed to succeed in tomorrow's workplace," according to their website. For the last several years, one hundred percent of the students participating in the program graduated high school, were accepted to college, and most of them graduated from college. The mentors provide personal support through high school with their time and effort while their organizations contribute to the financial support of running Aim High. The mentors for these students certainly helped contribute to making someone's life, and as a previous mentor, these students made our days and lives, too.

I've volunteered with Scouting throughout my life because of my own Scouting experiences as a youth and the values and skills I learned and still live by. My Scoutmaster, Mr. Gibson, had a huge impact on me. What youth organizations were you involved with growing up, and what lessons and values have stuck with you? Are you still involved in any way, even just sending them donations?

I've stayed involved with Scouting and music my whole life. With the heightened importance today of understanding, respecting, and being tolerant of differences, I worked with a team of volunteers to create a Walk of Faith (and during the pandemic a Virtual Walk of Faith) for all Scouts. For the virtual program, Scouts and families were introduced to five world faiths through a video, discussion, and online game and came away with greater knowledge and wonderful observations and appreciation for these faiths. It's the first program I've been involved with that had a perfect NPS (Net Promoter Score)—one hundred percent would recommend the program and would return. As we expanded it to other faiths, interest in the program more than doubled. Most recently we partnered with the Ebenezer Baptist Church in Atlanta to learn about their faith and storied history with Dr. Martin Luther King, Jr., whose father started the Troop for him. Many thanks to Ms. Black and Mr. King for helping make this a reality that brought interested Scout participants from coast to coast. This type of event may not have even been considered without the pandemic limiting us to holding Zoom-only experiences. It's so important to provide young people with the knowledge and insight to better understand and appreciate one another and, at the same time, make someone's day in the process.

You don't necessarily need special talents to make someone's day in a big way. My ninety-five-year-old cousin Flo in New York City still volunteers three times a week at a soup kitchen. The sight of her cheers many who come to the food kitchen, because she treats them all with respect. She wouldn't miss it, no matter what the weather. Food banks and soup kitchens need all types of help, including volunteers who are willing to listen to others, prepare or serve food, tell stories, or clean up.

Members of my professional association wanted to volunteer and help Chicago Public Schools (CPS), the country's second largest school district. I learned that CPS had a School Partners Program led by Dr. Santos to support the work of each school. We were matched with two schools. Members tutored at Cleveland Elementary School and others conducted a leadership in-service for the staff of Morgan Park High School. The members loved the opportunity to get involved with the schools and give back to the students, faculty, and community. These were services that the schools couldn't afford otherwise. And seeing the eagerness and talent of the volunteers made the day for the faculty and the students.

HELPING OTHERS WITH MOLECULES OF KINDNESS

Doing something in a big way doesn't have to be hard; it just could take some extra planning or organizing. My daughter Hillary, my sister Merril, and I love to volunteer and wanted to have a positive impact on others' lives after the devastation of Hurricane Katrina. We looked for a way to help rebuild homes and lives in New Orleans. Working through a church organizing the efforts, we were assigned to work on a home in the city. After working hard painting, drywalling, and sanding all day, we got a totally unexpected return. The person whose home we were rebuilding asked us if we wanted to go on a driving tour of the lower ninth ward. We said sure, and John took us to the area where the worst devastation occurred. Those homes were not being rebuilt because there was literally nothing left of them except the concrete steps that led to where the front door used to be. John showed us where the levees broke, the home of Fats Domino, and a part of the city history we would have missed since this wasn't the area where the rebuilding was occurring. In his way, he tried to repay us back, something that wasn't necessary. We were just trying to help rebuild his home and life. In return, he made our day by giving us a unique tour we would have never seen.

Dr. David Hamilton talks about "molecules of kindness" in his blog and book *The Five Side Effects of Kindness*. He says, "A molecule is a useful collection of atoms. I used to be an organic chemist so I made molecules every day." David was in a conference in Chicago and saw a number of homeless people, similar to those in many big cities who hit hard times. One person said to him, "I'm not looking for money. I'm just hungry and cold. Can you spare some food please?" He was touched by both the need and the honesty of the person. For the rest of the day, every time he saw a sign or heard a request like that, he stopped to buy a sandwich or something warm and offered it to the people asking. He says that we as people are genetically wired for kindness, and it's our deepest nature.

When Maureen goes out for breakfast, she doesn't forget the syrup. She always orders something that comes with a side of pancakes. But they're not for her. She asks for a to-go container with extra plasticware, butter, and syrup. Why? She gives it to the homeless. So why the syrup? When she gave her breakfast to one homeless woman, she was asked, "Do you have any syrup? Most people forget the syrup, and cold pancakes are dry to eat." She said, "Other people have given her pancakes, and they are often too dry. No one remembers the syrup and butter." Maureen now never forgets them.

We all know about organizations that provide meals to the needy, from soup kitchens to Meals on Wheels. There's an organization in Chicago that does this in a big way twice a year. They provide boxes of food for needy families during the holidays. People sign up anonymously (to protect their identity and self-esteem) and receive all the ingredients to create a festive holiday meal, no questions asked. People requesting a box do have to give contact information, but that's only used for delivery. The organization, Maot Chitim, delivers over five thousand boxes throughout the Chicagoland area to families who would not have a holiday meal without this help. Hundreds of volunteers help make this a reality by assembling boxes, banding the eggs, filling the boxes with non-perishable goods, adding the perishable goods to the boxes on delivery day, and loading the delivery trucks and cars of people who deliver these boxes to recipients in need. More often than not, the look on the face of the recipients is one of pure joy and gratitude. Talking with the recipients for a few minutes when delivering the boxes makes an even greater impression on them. Many don't speak English, so communication is basically nodding and smiling. There's that universal nonverbal, smiling!

EVEN CELEBRITIES DO IT

I was passing the ABC News studio in Chicago one summer day. The State Street studio is behind the front windows so people can watch the live news broadcasts. On this day, though, the shades were pulled down, perhaps because of the bright sun. Longtime newscaster, Ron Magers, was retiring that week, and two women had brought signs they were waving to get his attention. But with the shades down, no one could notice. I asked them what brought them there. They were sisters who took the day off to see and wish their favorite newscaster well in his upcoming retirement. But Ron Magers couldn't see the signs, and the glass was too thick for them to hear when I tried knocking. I suggested that we go into the lobby and ask the security guard if he could show Ron the signs. The guard said no and that we couldn't go in but added that Ron often takes a break between the local and national news. Just wait and he'll walk by. We waited twenty minutes after the local newscast with no Ron, and the sisters started thinking this would never happen. Just then the guard left, went back to the studio, and brought Ron out to meet his fans. The sisters were ecstatic. Just when they thought all was lost, they were able to greet him, take a photo with him, and make their day (and Ron's day!). I didn't know if I could help them, but why not give it a try? Otherwise, Ron would never know that some fans took time off of work to wish him well. Two years later, serendipity happened, and I ran into one of the sisters at a restaurant. She said how much that day meant to her and her sister and they would never forget it. This is what I mean when I say it may not be big or hard for you to do but it could be very meaningful for others. I knew there had to be a way to get Ron to see the signs and kept persevering until it happened.

Yo-Yo Ma is an outstanding musician and humanitarian. When getting vaccinated during COVID-19, he brought his cello with him so he could play for others to ensure they had some pleasant music while either waiting to get their shots or recovering from them. Just before COVID-19, he gave a free concert in Chicago's Millennium Park. An eleven-year-old fan, her mother, and her brother got to the park early enough to get seats to hear him, or so they thought. They were stopped by security and were told that the seating was full and they would have to wait until some people left. It didn't look full to them, so they waited.

And waited. People came and went, but they were still not allowed in. They were told those people had special passes or reserved seats. The family eventually left, disappointed, to say the least. The eleven-year-old fan decided she would write a letter to the editor of the *Chicago Tribune*. That letter was seen by someone with the Chicago Symphony, who asked the *Tribune* for the family's contact information. The Symphony then sent the letter and information to Yo-Yo Ma. Not too much later, this girl received a package in her mailbox. Inside she found a personalized note from Yo-Yo Ma, an autographed picture, and his latest CD. The note said, "This is what we played at Millennium Park. Hope you like it!" You think this girl will be a Yo-Yo Ma fan for life? A great example of hoping for one thing but then receiving something else from someone she will always admire for making her day.

Carola and Vittoria are two young eleven- and thirteen-year-old girls who made a sensation during the pandemic in 2020 by playing tennis on the rooftops of their buildings in Italy. One would be on one rooftop and the other across the street. The video of them playing went viral, and they talked about how they loved Federer. Enter their favorite player, Roger Federer. As they were doing what they thought was another TV interview, Federer showed up to surprise them and play a little rooftop tennis himself. The girls were ecstatic. The video showed them playing on one rooftop with Federer on another. Afterward, he took them out for some pasta. They kept saying they could not believe it. He said this was one of the more memorable moments in his career. That's awesome. Afterward, he sent them a video chat giving them a free scholarship to attend Rafael Nadal's summer tennis camp thanks to his sponsor. I'm sure he will always be their favorite tennis player. Here's the link if you'd like to see this yourself. https://www.atptour.com/en/news/federer-rooftop-tennis-july-2020

Basketball great Shaquille O'Neal is another star who likes giving back. There are many stories of his "random" generosity. Recently he was in a jewelry store where he overheard a young man struggling to pay off an engagement ring on layaway. Shaq simply told him, "I've got it covered. You've got other things to worry about." Shaq is particularly attracted to helping single young mothers struggling with providing for their children as it reminds him of growing up. He had only one new pair of shoes a year, and they were often several sizes too small. Shaq-to-School is a program that provides five thousand kids with school supplies. He believes kids gravitate to him because he relates to them. Shaq lives by the desire to always make someone's day in whatever way he can, often providing the financial means for something meaningful that others don't have.

Shaq is a giant both in size and in spirit. Mother Teresa is a diminutive giant and a Saint for her amazing dedication to serving the poorest of the poor in society, those in greatest need. Saskia was touched by Mother Teresa at age twelve and followed in her footsteps. She was introduced to her by her own mother, who volunteered in a soup kitchen run by Mother Teresa's order in Rotterdam, Holland. What cemented this connection was when her mother was asked to drive Mother Teresa to Amsterdam, and Saskia and her father joined on the car ride. She was so impacted by this experience that when Saskia was sixteen, she took a two-week school break and volunteered at Mother Teresa's orphanage in Calcutta. Saskia was immediately taken by the rawness of life in the street and the immense poverty and neediness of the people there. Even though Saskia did not speak the language, she felt the power of presence and making what she calls "pure connection" with the neediest, something Mother Teresa was able to do with everyone she met, from heads of state to the poor and homeless. Saskia described Mother Teresa as giving complete and undivided attention to anyone she was speaking or spending time with. When Saskia was asked to hold the hands of a dying woman, Saskia wasn't sure what to do since she didn't know the language. The hands felt cold, but Saskia learned the power of human connection from staring into this woman's eyes and being present. She learned about the need to be recognized as a person. The woman seemed to die at peace. This totally changed Saskia's perspective and life once more. When she graduated school, Saskia decided to dedicate her life to the cause of providing for the world's most misfortunate people with Mother Teresa's order. Making someone's day was her full-time job. Saskia said, "I learned so much from those that I was serving that I'm not sure if I was making their day or they were making mine." She certainly experienced the boomerang effect at the highest of levels.

FACING SERIOUS PHYSICAL CHALLENGES

My friend Ralph is a great bandleader, talented clarinetist and woodwind player, and music teacher. In a horrific freaky accident after a concert, a fixture from the ceiling fell right on him and shattered his spine. Fortunately, he survived this accident but now lives as a paraplegic with continuous care. When his daughter was looking for furniture for the twenty-four/seven caregivers he had to have, people donated both money and furniture. Musicians throughout Chicago organized a few benefit concerts for Ralph. Nothing can restore Ralph from his paralysis, but through these types of acts, we can make a difference to his life while entertaining others with spectacular music.

Do you know someone who has had life challenges and rose to meet them? There's a great story about a former paratrooper, Josh, who got injured and was told he would never be able to walk, confined to a wheelchair. Sounds similar to Ralph's story in a sense—a helpless situation except with a much younger person. By not moving or exercising, Josh gained hundreds of pounds. Doctors said there was nothing they could do to help him. Yet one medical professional years later believed differently. He said that Josh's life didn't have to be like this. One step at a time, literally, Josh fought back and started to lose weight and tried to walk. The miracle of being able to walk again happened only with much perseverance and dedication on his part and the encouragement and belief from the doctor who didn't believe in lost causes. Miraculously, Josh is back to the weight he started off as, out of a wheelchair, and able to walk. If someone believes in you, you can believe in yourself. Because almost anything is possible.

ESPN reported on August 8, 1982, about an athlete saving a child's life. A line drive foul ball screamed down the line and hit a four-year-old boy in the head at Fenway Park, home of the Boston Red Sox. His family were in seats close to the field, which now come with warnings to be on the lookout for foul balls. Jim Rice, one of Boston's star players, realizing that it would take EMTs too long to arrive and cut through the crowd, sprang from the dugout and scooped up the boy. He laid the boy, Jonathan, gently on the dugout floor, where the Red Sox medical team began to treat him. When Jonathan arrived at the hospital thirty minutes later, doctors said, without a doubt that Jim's prompt actions saved his life. Jim returned to the game in a blood-stained uniform. A real badge of courage. After visiting Jonathan in the hospital and realizing the family was of modest means, he stopped by the business office and instructed that the bill be sent to him. Nearly twenty-seven years after that game, ahead of Jim Rice's induction into the Hall of Fame, ESPN interviewed Jonathan and his dad. Remembering Rice's reputation as being somewhat stand-offish with the media, ESPN figured Rice would decline an interview request. Instead, according to Tom Keane, Rice replied, "I'll give you all the time you want. The most memorable moment in my baseball career was pulling the kid out of the stands of Fenway that day." Thanks to Jim's quick thinking and actions, he literally saved Jonathan's life and remembers that moment forever, calling it the most memorable moment in his hall of fame career.

LEVELS OF GIVING FROM KNOWN TO ANONYMOUS

The famous philosopher from the Middle Ages, Maimonides, said one of the highest levels of giving is to "give without knowing to whom one gives, and without the recipient knowing from whom s/he received help from." A story close to that level of giving is about Karen, who worked at the University of Notre Dame. Every day while driving home, she passed a billboard ad for someone desperately looking for a kidney. After consulting with her family, she decided to see if she was a match. She was! Karen talked with her boss about taking a short-term leave of absence to donate her kidney. He was totally on board and supported her efforts with whatever time off she needed. She was about to donate an organ to someone she didn't know—a total stranger—one of the greatest acts of selflessness you can do. Thank you, Karen, for being such a generous and kind soul. Your actions did more than make someone's day—you saved someone's life. And what's remarkable is there are many Karens out there who have done the same thing.

A recent app is called Buy Nothing. It's a sharing and giving community. You post something you don't need, and if someone is looking for it, poof, a match is made! Mo was flabbergasted when an old easel she had that was dirty and taped together was taken by someone when she posted it. The person said her daughter painted and didn't have an easel to use so painted her art on her kitchen table. The mom cleaned up the easel and gave it to her daughter that Christmas. Her daughter said this was her best present ever. Imagine that! Mo also gave away an old artificial Christmas tree to a family who said they now can celebrate Christmas for real every year with their own tree, which they never had. You're helping someone out you don't know and your only return is making someone's day—or holiday—happier!

GoFundMe is a great mechanism to help people anonymously in a significant way. GoFundMe is unique to crowdfunding in that they are not an incentive-based crowdfunding website. Although it does allow projects for musicians, inventors, etc., the business model is set up to allow for donations to personal causes and life events. The majority of GoFundMe pages help people with medical expenses. GoFundMe also has a special section dedicated solely to users who are trying to raise money to cover their tuition costs. One of the most notable tuition projects involved helping a user raise $25,000 to pay out-of-state tuition to a PhD program.

How else can you make someone's day without them knowing? There are many ways to do this that don't require you to donate an organ or pay a tuition bill. Start with small, simple actions like picking up litter. This may not help any one person in particular, but it does help people in general. Nature lovers call this "leave no trace." As a Scout leader, I frequently bring a bag with me on hikes to pick up stray cans and paper so others can enjoy nature trails undisturbed by litter. Several years ago,

I visited a national park in another country and was greatly disturbed to see trash—empty cans, bottles, and wrappers—left scattered on the trail. I picked up a few cans and bottles but didn't make much of a dent. It's a shame to see beautiful places like this spoiled. Making a little effort to pick up litter allows others to enjoy nature unblemished. If we all did that, there'd be no litter!

Besides picking up litter, here's another way you could help anonymously when shopping. Grab a stray shopping cart and put it in the cart corral. This may save someone from having the cart run into their car and cause a dent. Simple actions, big results, done anonymously.

Gigi is an older adult at Lambs Farm, a facility that serves developmentally disabled adults. Gigi loves Coke, and the cans cost fifty cents in the machine there. One of the people that works with Gigi purposely "drops" quarters, which Gigi loves to find to buy Cokes and always is excited when she finds one. Cyndi knew this would make Gigi's day by allowing her to find quarters. And Cyndi was equally excited to see Gigi happy. Small for Cyndi to do, large for Gigi. All of these efforts make someone's day, somewhat anonymously.

DONATIONS ARE NEEDED

Do you donate gently used clothes or household items to charity? Some people do so as a way of cleaning up clutter, others do it for the tax deduction, and others to help someone else in need. Don't just throw out unwanted but usable household items and clothes—donate them. Even your old car, whatever condition, can be given as a donation. This is another simple and big way to make someone's day easily while knowing in your heart you did the right thing.

Whatever your reason for donating, it coincides with a business model that is popular today: the sharing community. Whether cars or homes, rides or services, the sharing community that started with shared living space and transportation continues to grow and expand. Some of these "businesses" share for free while others are for profit ventures.

Couchsurfing (https://www.couchsurfing.com/) invites people into their homes and allows them to sleep on their couches for free. According to the website, "Couchsurfing is about sharing your life, your experiences, your journey, your home, your extra almonds or a majestic sunset. We believe that the spirit of generosity, when applied liberally, has the power to profoundly change the world." This is another example of helping make someone's day with some anonymity because you never know who the recipient is going to be, and the only cost is your hospitality and time.

Gardening is one of the top hobbies in the world. Many gardeners have such great success growing fruits and vegetables that they love to share their bounty with others. Some people give away their excess crop to pantries and homeless kitchens. Many different organizations welcome your extra fruit and vegetables, such as food banks, homeless shelters, community or seniors' centers, and home-delivered meal programs. AmpleHarvest.org has an extensive listing of different organizations throughout the United States that will accept extra produce. You can search for one near you on their website. FeedingAmerica.org also has a searchable listing of food banks throughout the US. What a great way to make someone's day anonymously while providing you the joy of gardening and raising a bumper crop.

Do you donate blood regularly? Those who do usually don't do so for anyone specifically but as a way to help others in need. It's truly a selfless (and healthy) act that literally saves lives. This is true any time of the year, but at holiday time, blood banks seem to run especially low. Here are six benefits of donating blood from the School of Health Science at Rasmussen College:

1) Giving blood can reveal potential health problems.
2) Giving blood can reduce harmful iron stores.
3) Giving blood may lower your risk of suffering a heart attack.
4) Giving blood may reduce your risk of developing cancer.
5) Giving blood can help your liver stay healthy.
6) Giving blood can help your mental state.

PUTTING INTO PRACTICE

There are so many ways to make someone's day in a big way, which just may require a little more planning and preparation. It doesn't have to cost you much except some time, your talent, and possibly some blood (or a kidney). And you can do so publicly or anonymously. Use Make Someone's Day to have the impact you want on your neighborhood, your community, even the world.

If you work for a company, find out if they support volunteering and get involved. It can be a one-time event such as a fundraiser or blood drive or a longer-term, ongoing effort. If not, consider making the case for your company to help a local organization. If you're self-employed or if your company is just not interested, explore where you'd like to make a difference that could use your skills, knowledge, and passion to make someone's day in a big way and get involved! Take a moment right now to make a plan for how you want to do this and what parameters to take into consideration (work schedule, family needs, etc.) And do something meaningful to you while helping others.

Throughout the book, I've referred to how managers and leaders can make someone's day in the workplace. The next chapter focuses completely on this and is helpful whether you're a leader, a manager, or an independent contributor.

CHAPTER 8

. . . .

MANAGERS AND LEADERS MAKING A DIFFERENCE AT WORK

"A good manager is a person who isn't worried about their own career but rather the careers of those who work for them." —H. S. M. Burns

GREAT BOSSES ARE ALL too rare. There's a saying that goes, "A truly great boss is hard to find, difficult to part with, and impossible to forget." I've had dozens of bosses and sadly can count the good ones on one hand. Incorporating Make Someone's Day at work can turn an okay boss into a good one and a good boss into a great one. Why not be the boss you want to be and can be? Show that you care, lead your employees to do their best work, and retain their talent and commitment to your organization. Treat your employees like the very important people they are by using the Make Someone's Day VIP Model with them and be memorable in a good way!

Glenn Llopis, author of the book *Leadership in the Age of Personalization* and a contributor to *Forbes* on leadership, wrote, "Great leaders are the most memorable. They go about their day leveraging their distinction by leading in ways that come most naturally to them. They are remembered and admired because they have their own unique style and approach that supports innovation and initiative and are known for making the workplace culture stronger, more unified and collaborative. The most memorable leaders always set the right tone. Their presence and charisma are in service to others and they go out of their way to make their employees feel secure. They embrace two-way communication and are active listeners. They observe the dynamics around them and take pride in staying ahead of the game. They are game changers and are constantly looking for ways to challenge the status quo; they identify and help course correct those who might bring the organization down and are quick to solve problems."

Let's look at specific examples of what some of the best and most memorable bosses do.

WHAT BEST BOSSES DO

One of my best bosses was enthusiastic, encouraging, and pushed me to higher levels. Kathy involved me in decision making, which motivated me and would often make my day. Just being involved and having a say made me feel that my ideas mattered. It wasn't pay or a better office, which are always nice but not of lasting value. It was about giving me what I needed, pushing me, encouraging me, listening to me, involving me in decision sharing, and allowing me to do the work that I loved. That's what I want from a boss and what I try to do and emulate as a leader.

Here's what Glenn Llopis said about his best boss: "My boss during my early corporate years was the most memorable leader I have ever worked for. Mark quickly and respectfully evaluated the organization, its talent, shortfalls, and the opportunities for growth. He recognized that the culture needed a refresh and renewed energy. He is the boss that helped shaped me into the leader I am today. He injected a renewed sense of professionalism in the organization and made others feel more relevant and important. He single-handedly used his unique leadership skills and capabilities to revive an organization that was growing complacent and needed some real leadership. I was grateful to have experienced the transformational impact of great leadership at an early age. It made me realize that people just want to be led the right way—where they feel valued and can contribute in meaningful and purposeful ways."

Llopis described characteristics of great bosses. I'll add examples for each of them.

1) **Authenticity. The most authentic leaders are the most memorable.**

Hubert Joly became CEO of Best Buy when they were experiencing trouble as other electronics stores were merging and going out of business. This was not the easiest of times to take over a business, especially a retail business Joly had no experience in. In his new book, *The Heart of Business*, Joly describes the eighteen inches between your heart and your brain as the most important distance in a person, saying, "Have an open heart and beginner's mind as you develop your leadership style." The first thing Joly did at Best Buy was to spend the week on the retail floor of a store in St. Cloud, Minnesota, reporting for work in khakis, the trademark Best Buy blue shirt, and a name tag that said "CEO in training." He wanted to have a beginner's mind and to see and hear from the workers on the frontline and from their customers what was going right and what wasn't. Afterward, Joly created an environment of transparency, celebrating even the smallest wins. This is not classic turnaround style where new leaders come in with their chopping block and cut headcount and stores. It was Hubert's belief in his people and his passionate leadership that turned the company around, without resorting to significant layoffs or closings. He lived the Make Someone's Day philosophy through inspiring his workers to greater success and performance and believing in them.

2) **Shares their wisdom. Memorable leaders enjoy sharing their wisdoms and secrets of success.**

Jan said her first boss in customer service was amazing. She would often invite her to listen to customer calls and explain what happened. Jan would then take the next call herself. She prepared Jan for every situation, customer, and project and then expected her to handle it on her own. She provided support while expecting that she produce good results. The job, like all jobs, had moments that were extremely frustrating, except Jan's boss gave her the resources to course correct, to understand what she did wrong and what she needed to do the next time so that Jan was continuously learning, growing, and improving. Helping you learn while letting go of control is a trait of a great boss.

3) **Does what others don't.**

Jack's best boss was also one of his first. "He was reasonable about workloads, provided insightful feedback and suggestions, and was always polite and professional in dealing with employees, colleagues, outside professionals, and clients. We knew he had our backs. And he dealt with problem employees with empathy and professionalism." That's key—to know and believe that your boss has your back. Honesty, support, consistency, and managing others the right way are signs of a great boss who believes in their staff and makes their day.

4) **Embrace the lessons of failure. Leaders that allow you to learn from failure are eager for you to grow and prosper.**

Sam's best boss was an attorney at a legal services firm. "My second day on the job, I made a random mistake, and when I turned in my work, I realized afterward that it was not what she wanted. I apologized profusely. You know what my boss said? She believed mistakes are made because of poor instructions, not poor employees, taking the guilt I had for messing up and instead turning it onto herself, saying her instructions were not clear enough. My respect for her grew both for that and many other things she did that made her a great manager and a great person. I have worked for many other attorneys, and none have earned my respect and steadfast loyalty the way she did." How many bosses do that, take on responsibility for a problem rather than blaming you? A great boss who takes responsibility for a mistake, an error, or a problem raises your spirits and makes you even more committed to your work.

5) **Gives you their valuable time and makes you feel valued.**

Some bosses are full of inspiration. Dave's best boss had this magic where he could just make you feel like you could do absolutely anything. "He instilled confidence like no one I've ever known. There is a lot of lip service every day to be a team player, but at the risk of sounding trite, he had a way of making you feel like you were an important and integral part of the team. What you did mattered to the company and to him. I don't have any idea how he did it. No effusive compliments, no empty praise, no weekly luncheons or gift cards. When he said, 'Thank you, I couldn't have done it without you,' you just knew he meant it." Dave's boss cared and trusted his employees and was honest and genuine with them. As a result, Dave became deeply loyal to his boss and was so motivated by him that he said, "I haven't worked for him in years, but if he needed a kidney, I'd see if I was a match." How many people do you know who feel that way about you or about their boss? Do you feel that way about *any* boss you've had? Dave's boss believed in his people and, in return, received great commitment, loyalty, and results.

6) **Creates special moments and leads to leave a legacy.**

My best bosses were positive, pushed me to grow, knew when something was critical and needed full attention, and knew when to ease up and have fun. They held memorable retreats and team building. They were attentive and upbeat. They checked in to see how I was doing, both at work and with my family. Simply put, they cared. And made sure we had fun at work through simple celebrations, not lavish ones. They wanted to make a lasting difference, and that made a difference to me.

What's common in these stories? No one said their boss paid the most, offered the greatest perks or bonuses. Stop and think about that. Best bosses are open, honest, and communicate fairly, clearly, and frequently. They want you to learn and continuously grow and improve. They trust and involve you in decision making and move toward what I call decision sharing. They take blame rather than shifting it to you and are genuine and effusive in their praise. They ask how they could help you and introduce you to their bosses and promote your work. They think about you and your family when they're away. They do all they can to make every employee's day, job, and career.

Preeminent organizational consultant Ed Schein has a new

book called *Humble Consulting* (2021). In it, he talks about the concept of levels of relationships. Ideally, we want to aim for a Level 2 relationship in organizations, a pragmatic one that is more than just being nice to one another. It's being humble and personal where each person is an equal partner in discussions and leads to better decision making through greater knowledge. Employees want to share what they know with their managers rather than hold back, and this additional information from those closest to the customer can make all the difference in making informed and shared decisions. This is the type of relationship where Make Someone's Day actions thrive.

MEANINGFUL WORK AND CULTURE FIT

Years ago, workers may not have had the same choices we have today. Many were told to "check their brains" at the door and follow instructions, especially those working on assembly lines. Not anymore, not if you want to be competitive and be an attractive employer. With Millennials and Gen Zs wanting more meaning from work and balance in their lives, what better way to make someone's day than to involve them in decision sharing, using their talents and capitalizing on their interests to strengthen their commitment to work?

A 2019 study from the Work Human Analytics and Research Institute called "The Future of Work is Human" has some relevant findings. "More than pay or free food or a fun team, workers are looking for meaningful work at organizations where they feel recognized and respected. Workers are more than twice as likely to recommend a friend when they agree that the work at their organization has meaning and purpose, and four times more likely to love their jobs if they connect with a sense of meaning and purpose." What a great way to make someone's day by having your organization's values and mission in alignment with what you believe and stand for. By recommending friends for positions who you know share those same values and beliefs, you are creating a workforce that feels the same way and in turn helping your organization find the right workers that are a match for their culture.

Many organizations see the importance of hiring someone who fits their culture as even more important than a skills match. You can train someone in the skills they may need for work; you can't necessarily train them to be a fit for your culture. We all know the organizations that do this well: Apple, Google, Southwest Airlines, Virgin Brands, Wegmans, Zappos all come to mind as strong cultures that have strong, customer-centered and employee-centered cultures as a key value. Their employees love their jobs and the values that these companies both espouse and live by.

This can be easier for nonprofits where employees are often inspired by their organization's mission and values, whether it's saving the environment, following your faith, education and learning, or healthcare, such as curing cancer. By choosing to work for these types of organizations, people are aligning their values and beliefs with where they choose to work and spend the majority of their time. Often the overall mission and purpose of these nonprofit organizations is to make someone's day every day.

Today we're even seeing this type of alignment in some business organizations. People can be motivated by the product such as healthcare and pharma (saving lives); the type of business, such as telecommunications or utilities (improved and better ways to communicate, keeping the power on); and even those companies serving consumers like you and me in hospitality and entertainment (who doesn't love Disney?!).

How do values and beliefs show up? Lisa was a partner in a branding and marketing agency responsible for business development. "I had received a referral to a very large potential client and was thrilled to go to the 'big meeting.' I had a long elevator ride in a high-rise office building, and when I stepped off the elevator, I heard a voice through the elevator shaft yelling for help. I was a bit shocked but decided to see what I could do. After talking with her and learning that she was trapped in another elevator for some time, I went and found the building manager to assist. I may have been late for my own meeting, but my values drove me to help someone in trouble. I then went on to my meeting, and the receptionist said my host was detained and was on her way in. After waiting for quite a while, my contact appeared and apologized for being so late, explaining that she was trapped in the elevator. After a great conversation around, 'That was you?' we ended up talking about kindness, and of course, I got the deal signed!" Lisa's value of helping others in trouble paid off, in this case with the contract she wanted. She unknowingly made her client's day by helping her out of a frustrating situation, and in turn her client made her day.

GRATITUDE AND RECOGNITION

Gratitude and appreciation can lead to higher levels of performance and lower stress levels. Chester Elton is known as the "Apostle of Appreciation" and has written several books with Adrian Gostick that highlight the importance of gratitude in the workplace. Showing appreciation to employees leads them to being twice as likely to trust and respect their manager and twice as likely to believe they can grow in the organization. Even more astounding is that employees can become five times less likely to lose engagement and disengage mentally from work when they feel gratitude. We're not talking huge bonuses here, just the act of gratitude and appreciation for the work you are doing.

Here's a great story from the *Washington Post's* Managing Editor, Tracy Grant. But it's not an article *in* the paper, it was something *for* the paper that was done by Marty Baron, former Executive Editor of the *Post*. Marty started receiving "a flood of notes, letters, and cards from readers around the world in 2016 expressing gratitude for our coverage" and who appreciated the hard work the *Post's* reporters and newsroom were doing. Readers wanted the writers and staff to know how meaningful their work was to them. Marty writes, "At some point early on, I thought I shouldn't be the only one to see these notes since readers were thankful for the work of our entire staff. We're accustomed to hearing only from the critics. I felt it was important to see what our supporters had to say and to know that there were many of them. And there also was something unusual about these notes. People were no longer taking the press for granted in our democracy. The writers of these notes wanted us to know that they had our backs and were rooting for us." Marty responded to every single note. And then he realized these cards weren't meant just for him, these notes of gratitude and appreciation were meant for everyone in the newsroom, all nine hundred to one thousand staff. Marty continues telling the story. "I never announced that I was posting these notes, but naturally word got around. And the window became a stop on many tours of the *Post*'s newsroom given by staff." And it wasn't a small window—it was a ten- to twelve-foot glass wall. As more notes came in, Marty kept adding them to the point that they covered the entire wall. According to Marty, "They had the desired effect: boosting the morale and fortifying the spirit of journalists who were so often pilloried for just doing their jobs well. I was enormously appreciative that readers wrote and that the notes had the positive impact I hoped for." Tracy Grant called them "love notes to us." Whenever someone on staff "needed to be replenished," they went by this "wall of gratitude" and read some of the notes. Many times they left with tears in their eyes. Knowing one's work matters and feeling appreciated is what many workers ache for. Prior to the pandemic shutting down the newsroom, Tracy made sure to take a copy of one of the notes that was most moving to her, so she could read it whenever she needed to be inspired. It's as if each card and letter writer shouted out, "You made my day!" to each person in the newsroom. What a fabulous way for a leader to share thanks and for readers (customers) to share their praise and inspire the whole workforce.

Make Someone's Day can be a great tool for every manager, leader, and team member to use to show appreciation. When asked what they would most like to change about their work culture, employees loudly proclaimed more appreciation from their bosses and their peers. When there are so many opportunities to recognize and appreciate employees, why do managers and bosses need to be reminded? Probably because they are focused on the work and the next task, which is what they're hired to manage and accomplish. But that's like saying to a child that grades are the only thing that matters in school. So much more learning happens at school, including socialization, teamwork, play, cooperation, and meeting deadlines. Likewise, so much more happens at work that is both on and off the job description. Bestselling author and consultant Ken Blanchard in *The One Minute Manager* said, "Catch your employees doing something right and offer them one-minute praise!" It doesn't take long or a lot of effort. Appreciation never goes out of style.

When leaders incorporate Make Someone's Day as part of their daily plan, it brings gratitude and appreciation to the forefront and keeps people motivated and excited about work. And it's not just for leaders! Everyone in your organization can contribute to appreciating each other and making someone's day a regular part of their work as well, creating a positive, reaffirming, and appreciative culture. Doing so builds an organization where people want to contribute, work hard, and stay. Why? Because people seek the qualities Make Someone's Day brings: appreciation, connectedness, growth, and to know that their work matters.

ONE SIZE DOES NOT FIT ALL

Yet like clothes, one size does not fit all. Appreciation can differ for each one of us. According to a Maritz, Inc. poll, only twelve percent of employees today say they get recognition that's meaningful to them, while thirty-four percent say, "The things that our company does to recognize people doesn't resonate with me." Here's a specific example where the right thing was done.

Michael is a keynote speaker, frequently speaking to organizations and large groups of managers. Often, the organization will give him a gift as a token of their appreciation. A nice gesture, but the item usually goes into a storage box and is soon forgotten. Except one time. On one occasion, Michael was asked to stay on stage after his talk to unwrap a gift. It turned out to be a coffee-table book, *Mountains of the World*. As he told me, "I'm a guy who loves mountains. I climb mountains, hike mountains, snowshoe on mountains, and simply am captivated looking at mountains. They almost had to drag me off the stage as I was scanning through the book! How did they know I love mountains? It turns out that six months earlier, when the meeting planner was reviewing the meeting details with me, she happened to say, 'Michael, what do you like to do when you're not consulting or speaking?' I responded, 'Mountains, blah, blah, blah . . .' Little did I know she was asking that with the intent of determining what they might get me as a thank-you gift. The reason I remember that experience so vividly is because the gift was tied to my personal interests. And when you give a person something tied to their personal interests, the message you send is that you care enough to find out who the person is and what's important to them. That's the power of knowing and doing something unique for each person."

Bob Nelson is considered one of the world's leading experts and speakers on employee motivation, engagement, recognition, and rewards. Dr. Bob likes to have and promote recognition and fun. His bestselling books include *1501 Ways to Recognize Employees, 1501 Ways to Reward Employees,* and his latest book, *Work Made Fun Gets Done!,* providing hundreds of non-monetary and even non-interactive ways to recognize, reward, and make someone's day at work. Dr. Bob said, "Most managers don't ask what employees want because they're afraid they're going to ask for more money, and maybe they will. But in my experience, that's typically not the response. They ask instead for more flexible working hours, or a software upgrade, or to present results of their work to the management team." These are simple and meaningful ways to recognize employees and make their day. Many don't cost much. Let's look at some other no- and low-cost ways to show appreciation and learn how you can make someone's day at work.

Putting flowers or a plant on someone's desk before they arrive or sending them to virtual workers is simple, effective, and usually greatly appreciated. Decorating a desk, leaving a note, or sending an e-card can also have a big impact and can be done so by an individual, a team, or anonymously. That provides fun and is meaningful to the person receiving it and often makes their day.

Working virtually? Maybe there's a virtual badge you can award that your staff can include in their signature. When workers started working remotely during the pandemic, some companies went out of their way to make sure people had all the technology and supplies they needed. Above and beyond that, some organizations sent a gift card for a local restaurant to members of their team. My sister Merril received one and was greatly appreciative. It's the little, thoughtful things you do that make a difference, keep loyalty, and make someone's day.

Another element of remote working was people got to know each other's families more. Interruptions that may not have been tolerated before the pandemic became welcome insight into someone's life, making us all feel more connected. Anyone been zoomed in with a cameo from a precious pet or seen the BBC broadcaster interrupted by his young child coming into the room during a live broadcast?! There's something about opening up our personal world to the people we spend the most time with—our colleagues at work—that creates more affinity toward one another. And greater knowledge allows us more insight to make someone's day.

JUST SAY THANK YOU

What's even easier than sending something? Saying thank you. Those simple words make such a difference because too often at work we don't say it and people wonder, "Have we done this right? Is this appreciated?" Saying thank you and letting people know why they are appreciated helps them know they are on target and encourages them to repeat this behavior in the future. Saying thank you is so easy to do online in an email, a thumbs-up in person, or best, a comment speaking specifically to the person's accomplishment.

Which is what Doug Conant did through handwritten thank-you notes. Who doesn't like acknowledgement from a boss, especially the top boss? Doug became CEO of Campbell's Soup when there was more than tomato soup in the red. He describes in his book *Touchpoints* what he did to turn around the company. One of the key elements was personally writing two hundred to two hundred fifty notes every week to managers and staff throughout Campbell's praising them for something they did. Doug points out it's the smallest of actions that make the biggest difference in motivating leaders and employees. Can you imagine the power of receiving one of these notes that the CEO heard or noticed something you had done well? Let alone what about the time learning enough to write hundreds of specific notes every week? What a great way to create a positive culture. I'm always pleased when I get a note from a boss or client and often save them. It makes you realize people do notice and that you make a difference. What an easy and awesome way to tell someone you made my day! Or, as Doug Conant learned, turn around a culture and a company. Mmmm, good for you, Doug.

Another way to do this is sending or cc'ing a note (cc means carbon copy from the days of typewriters and carbon paper) to a person's boss. Nothing is better than having the boss hear how well an employee is doing. Typically, managers are asked to write examples of the actions and results their employees did in the past year for their performance reviews. Managers frequently have trouble coming up with enough positive examples in part because we work in a matrixed or team environment where interactions between manager and employee are less frequent. Or we're working remotely and they just don't know. These notes can provide the specific feedback and compliments that are both greatly appreciated by the employee and can be most useful by the manager to reference in the formal appraisal process.

Does writing a note really make a difference today? My stepson Jacob got a note from the partner in charge at his accounting firm where he worked as an industrial consultant. He had been working on a new program out of town for several days with little sleep because they were going live with a new system for a large client. The partner called out Jacob's work in a thank-you and copied the whole executive suite. Can you imagine how motivated Jacob felt? What type of effort do you think he'll put in if he had to do that again?!

LOVE WHAT YOU DO—IT SHOWS

Do what you love and love what you do. Maybe what you love is not what you do but how you do it. For example, you may love interaction with people where the work is secondary to the contact that you have with others throughout the day. My mom Sally loved several of her jobs for both the public contact and the perks. She worked at Marshall Field's, a Chicago-area department store, in Evanston part-time, because she liked the interaction with customers and the discount from the store. Each night she would happily tell us who she ran into or tempt us with delicious desserts from the store bakery. (That wasn't too hard to do!) It didn't matter to Mom which department she worked in as long as she was able to see and talk to people each day. She later became a travel agent because she loved to travel. As a travel agent, I was amazed that my mom in her fifties, sixties, and seventies would learn a new travel operating system when she changed travel agencies or they changed providers. She loved the opportunity to take very low-cost "fam" tours where she'd travel to new or exotic places with other travel agents, visiting hotels, restaurants, and sightseeing venues. It was the combination of helping others, the contact, and the perks that excited her about these jobs. By working at jobs she loved, she always made the day for her customers, who in turn loved working with her.

After working a corporate job, Barry decided to work closer to home and opened up a local hardware store, which he ran for ten years. He loved building and fixing things, and his customers were very loyal because he was so knowledgeable and helpful. A big box home improvement store moved in and took too much of his business, so he had to close down. He then went back to an IT corporate job before retiring. After several months in retirement, he decided he's much happier helping people fix things. He now works at another local hardware store, to the delight of his former customers, who always loved his help and advice on repairs and home improvements.

The late jazz impresario Joe Segal in Chicago occasionally had to ask the musicians he hired for cab fare home because business was so slow that he could barely afford to pay them. But he was passionate about jazz and introduced the music he loved to small and large audiences at the Jazz Showcase, where the biggest acts used to play when they came to town. He created "save the children" matinee performances on Sundays, where children twelve to eighteen could come for free, making their day by hearing great jazz artists and his day by creating a new generation of jazz fans!

LIFESTYLE AND BEING THERE
MAKE A DIFFERENCE

With so many people discovering the joy of working remotely from home, we may be better able to meet both professional and personal needs in this way. I moved into consulting because I read Geoff Bellman's book *The Consultant's Calling*. He talked about the independent lifestyle of working from home as an equally important part of his decision as the work he did, which resonated with me. As someone who always believed that home needs never stop nor does thinking about work, I've always liked to blend both whenever I could. Being able to do so through working virtually makes my life and work more satisfying and led me to often combine both when I could, such as visiting friends and family before or after business trips when I travelled. Because of reading Geoff's book and understanding more of what it was like to be a consultant, he made my day and helped lead me to this profession.

Mary is an HR leader for a small suburban city. She was in a virtual meeting, and afterward, she received an email from one of the participants. "He said that just seeing my smile and hearing my laugh turned a day that wasn't going so well in the other direction. This is just another example of the many ways each and every interaction we have with others has an impact. And it made me feel good, too!" This is why I talked about showing up in chapter five—it means more than you think, and too often you don't even know it.

FUN AND HUMOR AT WORK

When I think of fun at work, I think of the fish philosophy. If you've ever been to the Pike Place Market in Seattle, they make buying fish fun. When a customer comes in and tells them what fish they want, they pick it up from the ice keeping it fresh and throw the fish around to each other, yelling funny things as these fish "fly" from one worker to another, eventually landing at the worker who wraps it up for the customer. They are the main attraction at the Pike Place Market and have become so popular they created the Fish philosophy focused on these four steps: 1) Be Present. 2) Play. 3) Make their day. 4) Choose your attitude.

These elements are all important in making someone's day as well. 1) Be present. Make someone's day happen because people notice. They are aware and see or hear things that lead to making a difference. 2) Play. If you can instill fun with work, you'll enjoy it much more. Have fun with what you do. 3) Making their day is what this book is all about. 4) And when you choose to make someone's day, you're choosing your attitude.

Here's a playful example. I was teaching a presentation skills class in Alaska to National Park Service superintendents and mentioned that I hadn't seen much wildlife that time of year (it was early spring) and thought they were probably still hibernating. The next day, I heard some sounds in the elevator, and a Park Ranger walked in with his pet llama so I would be sure to see wildlife in Alaska! Does he know how to play and have fun? You bet! It's all about adding variety and fun to life. Lightening the mood allows us to make someone's day. The Ranger sure knew how to make mine!

A Robert Half International survey found that ninety-one percent of executives believe a sense of humor is important for career advancement while eighty-four percent believe that people with a good sense of humor do a better job. A study by the Bell Leadership Institute found that the two most desirable traits in leaders were a strong work ethic and a good sense of humor. Deadlines and priorities are one thing. Keeping things light with levity and humor makes the workplace fun and puts everything in perspective. Sharing a joke or finding something funny during a tense moment in a project provides relief when it's most needed. It can make someone's day by releasing some of the tension we feel when we're caught up in the work and a tight deadline.

I was Skyping to some friends in Germany who asked how this book was coming, and Philipp asked, "What's the name of the book?" I told him, "*Make Someone's Day.*" He had a furrowed look on his forehead and looked quizzically at me sincerely and asked, "Why did you write a book about 'make some mistakes?'" I just laughed and said, "I'm sure all of us need to make some mistakes and share what we learned from them, but that's not what this book is about. This is *Make Someone's Day*, and you just made mine!"

Alan knows how to have fun at work. "We were planning a pancake breakfast for our department and families. Jean shared that fifty-seven adults and seventeen kids were coming. I was concerned about the parking, so I wrote back, 'How many cars?' I hoped that she would read that as, 'How many households?' and give me that number, assuming one car per household. Jean wrote back, 'Are the cars big pancake eaters?' I thought about this for a while and wrote back later that evening mentioning all types of cars named after animals: 'Well, Jean, the impalas love pancakes, as do the broncos, mustangs, and pintos. Get enough beetles down there, and they will devour a few. The stingrays and marlins couldn't care less. The skylarks and thunderbirds will just pick at them. The cobras and vipers will squeeze down a few each. And the jaguars will come to feast on all the others.' Jean wrote back to me, 'The visual image here is truly marvelous. You made my evening.'"

PUTTING INTO PRACTICE

Have you had fun at work, even just sharing a joke or a funny story with a coworker? Think of a time at work that was particularly fun. It could be a story or a celebration, activity or event. What was it and what did that do for you? How can you help repeat it or make it better? Volunteer to do so!

PERKS AND BENEFITS THAT MEAN SOMETHING

Offering a perk helps, too. Perks come in many forms, and earlier I mentioned two that my Mom liked, a store discount and travel. Attending a learning event or conference has always been a great perk for me. When I started my career, I had the chance to go to seminars to hear people I greatly admired, such as Malcolm Knowles (the father of adult learning) and Gifford Pinchot III (who created the concept of intrapreneurship). I had read their books and was delighted to meet and hear them in person. This was over forty years ago, and I still have vivid memories of it. That made my day and strengthened my desire to stay in a learning career.

Other "perks" include working on special projects. I was asked to co-lead a team at my first job to develop a program on career development and coaching. That had been an interest of mine since graduate school and was something I had dreamed of doing. It took eight years until the company was ready to support this, so it didn't happen overnight. I spent over a year creating the program and had the opportunity to hire and work with Marilyn Moats Kennedy, a career expert who I had long admired. That in itself was terrific. To top it off, I worked with a video development team in Toronto and got to meet and interview some terrific actors in the film. We filmed a welcome from the CEO, which was my first personal exposure to him, another highlight. The Being Your Best project made my day and allowed me to give back a program that would last for many years and impact thousands of employees. I was ready to leave the job a few years before this project and am so glad I stayed. This project kept me engaged and excited and had a profound impact on my career.

Have you had any special projects you've been involved with, served on an interdepartmental team or task force, or won an award or recognition for something you've accomplished? These all make you feel like your contribution to work is very important and go beyond the day-to-day aspects of the job. Whether it's a departmental or company task force or company or professional award and recognition, they are all worthy and may even lead to access and exposure to executives and other areas of the company you may not normally encounter. When I won a professional award from my association for Staff-Volunteer Partnership, I sat in the "green room" with Oscar Arias Sanchez, a past president of Costa Rica and Nobel Peace Prize winner. It was spectacular just to meet him. It's these asides that can make our day in the biggest of ways.

A LITTLE EXTRA EFFORT CAN MAKE A BIG RETURN FOR VOLUNTEERS

When I was chair of my professional association chapter and in leadership roles in other organizations, I instituted Return on Board Member Investment to recognize and reward board members for their time and effort. It took some planning on my part and learning what motivated my board or committee members. Often the reward was little gifts, learning events, or introducing them to the right connection or author. My largest effort was when I matched my committee members to board members of my professional association, finding the best match for each pair by geography, interests, or industry. This had never been done before, and as we were walking into the board meeting where I was going to present this idea, Rob, the board chair, asked me, "Do you really think it will work?" I believed that it would, which was why I took the extra time to match each partner around shared professional interests or geographic location to each other. It turned out that board members were thrilled to learn more about the association from my NAC (National Advisors for Chapters) committee members, and the chance to have such a personal connection for my committee members shot up their productivity as a result of this connection. And the association benefited because board members had a more personal understanding of local chapter needs. Since the pairing happened virtually, when they finally met each other at our association's annual conference, they felt they were long-lost friends. Multiple Make Someone's Day moments happened as a result.

EDUCATION AND LEARNING AS A PERK

Appreciation often doesn't involve money, but if it does, it usually benefits both you and the organization. Tuition reimbursement is one of those two-way benefits—the employee earns a degree and the company gets someone with greater skills and expertise. The payback is also great for attending or speaking at industry and professional conferences, going to workshops, and gaining certifications. The return the company gets is a more knowledgeable, committed, and motivated worker. In the television reality show *Undercover Boss*, many times it's the CEO at the end providing financial help to workers to complete their education or cover medical illnesses of family members that causes the most tears and brings the most joy. Make Someone's Day moments.

A college was going through some tough times financially and had to hold the budget steady for several years, which meant no raises for staff. People cried out for learning and growth at least. Senior leaders decided they could invest in leadership training for staff, emphasizing new leadership and collaboration skills. The program exceeded expectations, breaking down silos, creating new partnerships, and motivating staff who had stayed through the tough times. Leaders were able to grow and collaborate with one another, which made a difference for them and for the students at the school. It worked in another way as well. The first people who came to the program worked on the frontlines. They became very enthusiastic, embracing the concepts and collaborating with other people and departments in ways they hadn't before. Making someone's day became the norm, and when it came time to decide if they wanted to expand the program for a second year, the answer was an unequivocal yes.

As part of the leadership program, I created a service-learning process where participants practiced the leadership skills they were learning as a volunteer for a service organization or special project. This allowed them to get greater competence and confidence in their newly learned skills and created a double win: a win for the leader in applying and developing their new skills and a win for the organizations to get volunteers with skills they needed. Examples include one charity that raised more money from their annual golf outing than ever before as a result of a leader practicing his new finance knowledge and a child's art exhibit of the future of medicine ("Through the Eyes of a Child") that better connected the school with the community and increased visibility.

Informal mentoring and coaching can help as well as Neville describes. "It is great when you have a quiet word of support and advice to someone who weeks later thanks you for it. Having asked them questions to help them identify the root cause of their discomfort, we explored options. A single focus was agreed. They have since started to really contribute well. It was satisfying to watch them grow, but they made my day when they sought me out a month or so afterward to simply thank me. I believe that we can give freely. If we can enable people to more consistently enjoy performing at their potential, it can bring enjoyment to both parties. It is good to enjoy other people's success. The support doesn't have to come through any formal mentoring or coaching but in this case through sharing professional insight in a simple and memorable way. Seeing them show joy at having improved their performance progressively in the intervening weeks and setting new standards of expectation and results was fabulous. This happened just because they asked."

THE VALUE OF RITUALS AND CELEBRATIONS

In insurance companies and other professions, continuing education is highly encouraged. As a result of completing an insurance designation, which requires taking and passing a series of exams that take several years to finish, graduates at Allstate were given a free trip to the annual conference where confirmation was taking place. People timed their completions to attend some fabulous locations. My colleague Malcolm didn't get his dream trip when he completed the arduous, ten-part exam. He ended up receiving his designation in St. Louis, just several hours from home rather than a vacation spot. No matter, he was so pleased and proud that he completed his designation that he enjoyed himself learning and being recognized at the conference. That made his day.

Rituals can also make someone's day. Here's a crazy thing we did when I worked in executive education. Every time we got a new client, we "croaked" the frog, a plastic frog with a button you turned on to hear it croak. Frogs had become our theme because of our name, LEAP, and it was an honor to be able to "croak the frog." With its loud "ribbit" sound, other staff in the school would hear and gather to learn about our latest client and program offering. It sounds nuts, but when you've worked hard and have a chance to share it with others, it feels good to do so. It made each one of our days when we croaked the frog to share our news. Do you have any traditions at your company? If not, start one!

How about recognizing an individual or team completing a special project with a team party to acknowledge their success? Even if the party is a potluck, taking time out to celebrate the accomplishment can make everyone feel good about their contribution and work. These are simple ways of demonstrating how people matter and can make their day.

Company awards and honors can also be motivational. My daughter Hillary worked at a small startup and got to take some special seminars where she was able to benchmark with others in her field. She got some very helpful feedback about how well she was doing.

Many people enjoy earning special certifications for assessment, to teach courses, or to coach. These opportunities definitely made their day and gave them new expertise.

I've volunteered throughout my career with my professional association, ATD, feeding my desire to continue to learn and grow and in the process hearing some amazing authors. I talked about reading Geoff Bellman's book, *The Consultant's Calling*, that led me to the work I love to do. Geoff asked to speak to my chapter when he was promoting a new book, and it was an honor to finally meet and make friends with him. I've reached out to him for advice several times in my career. I met another mentor of mine, leading coach and consultant Marshall Goldsmith, several times as well, and when talking to him after a keynote address and he asked me if I wanted to hear him at a seminar the following weekend in New York, I jumped at the chance. Since then, I have become a part of the Marshall Goldsmith MG100, a group of outstanding senior executives and coaches who are all learning and continuing Marshall's work. The people you meet can have a powerful impact and make your day or, as with Geoff and Marshall, have a lifetime impact as mentors and role models.

USE THE VIP MODEL AS A MANAGER AND LEADER TO MAKE SOMEONE'S DAY

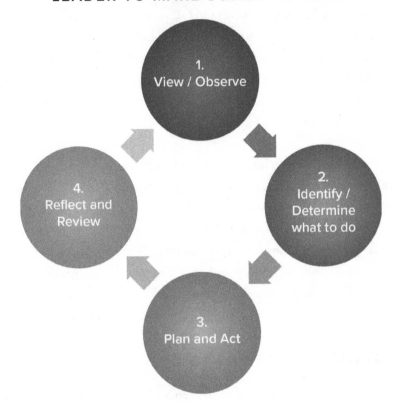

As a manager or leader, how can you apply the VIP Model and use this knowledge to make your staff and colleagues' day at work? Here's a reminder.

1) **V**iew/observe/discuss with your staff what they'd like to learn and do. In your conversations with your staff, discover what work interests and excites them the most and what recognition they most prefer.

2) **I**dentify opportunities for them to learn and apply their knowledge and skills. Match opportunities, projects, and goals your organization has with your staff's interests and developmental needs. Their motivation to do the work will be at its highest when you do so.

3) **P**lan with them the actions they need to take and agree on expectations and support they may need. Afterward, recognize them for their

accomplishments. And don't forget to find out what motivates your staff and colleagues. If they don't know or you need a different idea, give them Bob Nelson's book *1501 Ways to Recognize Someone at Work*. Bob said some managers even pass the book around to have all their staff identify how they want to be recognized and rewarded.

4) **R&R** Afterward, be sure you review what worked and what you would do again either with them or with others. Continually learn and refine your use of the model.

Treat the people who work for and with you like a VIP. Chances are if you offer a project or learning opportunity that interests your employees and reward and recognize them in a way that matters to them when they are successful, they will continue to give back to the job with greater loyalty, commitment, effort, and pride. These qualities are in short supply in organizations today and go a long way toward providing the energized workforce many organizations seek. This makes their day and your company's day and leads to you becoming a better boss.

PUTTING INTO PRACTICE

As a manager or leader, Make Someone's Day is one of the best tools you have to motivate, excite, and encourage people to perform at their highest level and for you to be seen as a best boss with their interests in mind. Be a great and memorable boss by following the characteristics. Remember that everyone is different, no one size fits all, so be sure to specifically identify projects that are motivating and helpful for people and recognize them in the way they would prefer. You'll discover that time spent planning and doing this right will pay big dividends.

If you manage or lead anyone, identify specifically how you can use the VIP method to make their day. Identify the person, their desires and interests, and their preferred recognition. Plan to do this in the next week, and if you're a leader, take time to do this for everyone on your team.

In chapter nine, we move to what we have learned in a crisis.

CHAPTER 9

· ·

WHAT WE HAVE
LEARNED IN A CRISIS

"In every crisis, doubt, or confusion, take the higher path—the path of compassion, courage, understanding, and love." —Amit Ray

THE PANDEMIC OF 2020 cancelled most public holiday celebrations in the US, including Memorial Day. CBS News' *On the Road* correspondent Steve Hartman partnered with retired Air Force bugler Jari Villanueva to create "Taps Across America" and keep the spirit of the holiday alive, honoring our veterans. As reported on the CBS Evening News on May 22, 2020, "Hartman and Villanueva asked veterans, musicians, teachers, and students of all abilities, ages, and instruments to sound Taps on their front lawns, porches, and driveways at three p.m. local time on Monday, May 25, 2020. Taps is the somber twenty-four-note bugle call played at American military funerals, ceremonies, and scout campfires. Hartman and Villanueva hope that the nationwide event will offer an opportunity to pause for a moment to pay tribute to fallen service members and victims of the coronavirus pandemic while maintaining social distancing guidelines." Remarkable and what a great way to involve the whole country. I joined in and played Taps on my sousaphone in our driveway, as well as a few patriotic songs. This is an event that may outlive the necessity for it when the pandemic is over because so many people can become involved right from their homes and make the day of veterans in their neighborhoods.

Natural disasters and global diseases, such as the pandemic, affect many people. Sometimes a crisis gives us a chance to do something for others that truly makes their day and their life. These can range from the simple (playing taps) to the extraordinary, such as the work of some countries that send emergency services and relief teams to help regions recover from natural disasters, like Doctors Without Borders.

HELPING OTHERS IN TIME OF NEED

During the start of the coronavirus pandemic, a number of seniors and elderly people couldn't get out to the store to get vital medications and food. Many young people offered to help them out by doing the errands for them. They posted flyers in their neighborhoods and went door to door to let others know they can help. They wouldn't accept any payment or tips for doing this. That's beautiful, caring, and community-minded. Here's just one example of a college student who went even farther.

When University of Alabama student Michael Arundel's classes were halted because of the pandemic, he returned to his family's home in suburban Orland Park outside of Chicago in the spring of 2020. "I think we were all looking for something to do during this time, and I heard about the need for seniors to get critically needed medical supplies and food. I felt helping them out would be the best use of my time," he said. To that end, Arundel started a group called Leave it to Us, a no-fee shopping service for senior citizens who were underserved and didn't feel safe going out to the store. He said to elderly neighbors, "You call me and I'll talk to my friends and see who wants to step up for the day and go shopping. There are no fees involved." Reflecting on doing this, Michael said, "It makes you feel better inside. You're not sitting there and watching Netflix and just kind of being bored. You're actually impacting somebody in a great way, and you're doing it safely." As of this writing, his initiative had grown to thirty-five chapters of Leave it to Us throughout the US, as its popularity has taken off and grown. Bravo, Michael and all of those who have helped!

Other people who had a bit of an abundance offered to give away things such as extra toilet paper (a valuable item when the pandemic started for some reason) and paper towels to those who needed it. Some people tried to take advantage of others by stocking up on needed supplies and then price gouging. A number of them were stopped or caught by police. Fortunately, generosity far surpassed those that were selfish.

The city of Highwood, Illinois, usually has summer festivals and events that raise donations and food for those in need. Celebrate Highwood had to find a different model during the pandemic. "We raised $4,000 from the community in literally two days and were able to feed over two hundred families," said Celebrate Highwood spokeswoman Ilyse Strongin in the *Chicago Tribune*. They then developed partnerships with corporate sponsors, restaurants, and the community to meet the needs of even more people. "One catering company brought trucks filled with bags of groceries containing produce, cheese, greens, meats, and eggs. Another restaurant started cooking warm steak tacos at seven a.m. to feed recipient families in line. Organizers said that for a donation of fifteen dollars we can provide three pounds of rice, three onions, five pounds of tomatoes and potatoes, and two pounds of chicken." Making someone's day by providing essential food for families in need.

As a school social worker, my stepdaughter Annie loves to do things for others in the community. During the pandemic, some homeless shelters put people up in very low-cost hotels so they would stay more socially distanced, but they still had to get food to them. Annie and my wife Laurie put together brown bag breakfasts as a way to give back and help those in need.

Vaccine angels helped people get vaccine appointments. Because of the haphazard way people had to sign up online for vaccine appointments in the US, many people and especially older people were at a disadvantage. They did not have success or the know-how to be online at the various odd hours when appointments were released, sometimes before dawn or very late at night. Annie, her brother Ben, and her friend Paula helped maneuver through this "data jungle" to find and make thousands of appointments for those that couldn't navigate the system themselves. To many, they were angels in helping get through the process and frequently were able to even find appointments in people's own neighborhoods. The gratitude and appreciation people expressed afterward was most touching and certainly made Annie's day after she made theirs with finding appointments.

LaTasha Murray works in health care as the marketing director for Robeson Health Care Corp., an organization that generally serves lower-income and historically marginalized communities, including her home of Red Springs, North Carolina. In a story reported on NBC, LaTasha said she has "made it her mission to raise awareness about the vaccine among her neighbors, and to make sure that they're basing their decision as to whether they were going to get vaccinated on facts, and not fiction." Now, wherever Murray goes—Walmart, the post office, the laundromat—she brings up the vaccine. "You literally cannot have a conversation with me without me talking about it," she said. "I was going to get a T-shirt that said 'vaccine hustler.'" It's personal, emotional connections like Murray's that are proving to be a driving force of vaccinations in many communities. While some are worried about conspiracy theories, many others simply have questions about the shots. How were they made? How were they developed so quickly? Will the shots hurt? "This became very personal for me," she said. Murray's calming presence has played a major role in her community members who call her day and night, asking her to go with them to their appointment and hold their hand. "Are you gonna meet me there?" they ask, and Murray always answers without fail, "Yep, I'll be there. I'm on my way." Making their day.

Many others stepped up in the community to meet the needs of others. The neighborhood app Nextdoor created a new button called "help needed" at the top of its page where people could post requests of needed services, from picking up prescriptions and groceries to pet care and other items. People using the app then volunteer to do the errand while they're doing their own errands.

Many food safety training vendors such as A+, Always Safe Food

Group, and State Food Safety started offering free training in sanitation and even basic home food safety for people who were cooking at home much more. Some provided this free training to restaurant owners during the pandemic, such as A Plus Food Training who offered free courses through Chicago area chambers of commerce. State Food Safety also added numerous classes, including Hand Hygiene, COVID-19 Safety Training for Food Operators, COVID-19 Safety Training for Apartment Managers, COVID-19 Safety Training for Pool Operators, Food Safety for Charitable Feeding, Food Safety for Disaster Relief, Food Safety in Real Life (YouTube), and Food Safety Talkabout (YouTube). And the Always Safe Food Group made sanitation training available to all.

STEPPING UP IN UNUSUAL WAYS

Other people have gladly shared their professional expertise for free, from coaching aspiring movie makers by filmmakers who had to stop shooting documentary films, to teaching music lessons and helping children with remote learning. There's even support and outreach for those who need help with their pets. The generosity of people during challenging times absolutely makes people's day.

"I have some disabilities. I'm immunosuppressed," said a retired registered nurse trying to help others in the pandemic. Working behind the scenes, she would call local pharmacists in town to see if they were delivering free of charge or offering curbside pickup. She posted those details, plus information about medicine availability. Even with challenges, she was making life easier for others and making their day.

BRINGING PEOPLE TOGETHER

"Fighting for a common cause obviously brings people together," says Talya Steinberg, a psychologist in private practice in Santa Fe, New Mexico, and an adjunct professor of counseling at Southwestern College. Because the pandemic is global, she says, "we actually are all facing the same catastrophe. This is unprecedented. If we are all in the same boat, we need to help each other." So there's something unprecedented about this particular crisis of the pandemic, but all crises seem to bring people together, supporting one another, and making each other's days.

Do you like to sing? When people are keeping their distance from each other, that's challenging. Sofa Singers was created to give people an outlet to enjoy singing with others around the world, all online, "to spark joy and human connection." Set up by vocal leader James Sills as a response to global self-isolation during the coronavirus outbreak, the Sofa Singers bring together hundreds of people in real time worldwide for forty-five minutes of simultaneous singing, learning a classic song with some optional harmonies/backup parts.

A small group of people who worked out at the Lakeview Fitness Center in Vernon Hills didn't know how they were going to work out during the pandemic. They contacted one of the instructors, Anne, who started off writing out exercises for them to do. Someone suggested that they could do them live on Zoom. Anne loved the idea and started right away, somewhat selfishly because she knew she would get her own workout in if she had to teach a class. And she said to herself, "I can do my little part in this crummy situation when we're all stuck at home. Why not exercise together?" What's more, she offered these sessions for free. So did Felicia through Facebook Live. Felicia also had exercise students contacting her about what they could do, and she discovered she could do classes two to three times a week on Facebook Live and time them so her daughter, who was working ninety hours a week as an ER nurse, could participate. It started off with just the people she knew and grew from there. After classes resumed in person, both instructors kept their online classes because they both had strong followings outside of the community. In fact, Felicia is back full time but still records her workouts on Instagram for others to follow, and she ended up with people in Australia and France following her workouts. Anne has kept her early morning classes going on Zoom and plans to do so indefinitely. At its height, over fifty people attended these classes. Anne and Felicia not only made people's days, they did their best to keep people in shape during the pandemic.

Valentina is CEO of a foundation that brought her staff together in a different way to boost their spirits during the pandemic. They scheduled an online game night for all staff. Fun, right? Cody, the VP of HR, wanted to do even more. So he drove to everyone's home and dropped off snacks, prizes, and some bubbly so they could all enjoy game night in style. That thoughtfulness by Cody, who hadn't met anyone since he was hired during the pandemic, ensured that the game night would be a big success, and it was bringing the team together in a way that made everyone's day.

FOOD ALWAYS HELPS

Morag described how snacks had always been an important part of her team meetings at work. "Whether over a meal, a drink, or simply a donut, snacks have brought us together. When we were thrust into the work-from-home environment, I realized that we would need to find a new way to come together during our (virtual) meetings to maintain old habits. I registered each of my team members for a service that delivers a different snack box each month from around the world. It has brought us closer together. It made their day the first time the surprise package arrived and rekindled that excitement each time a new box was delivered. The feeling of receiving the gift, curiosity to see what snacks have been included, and the laughter as we share our likes and dislikes was great. This is one of the ways we've kept our culture while continuing to work remotely."

COMING TOGETHER TO LEARN AND PRAY

Out of struggles and challenges, people become closer with one another despite keeping social distance. Many houses of worship transformed to online services and classes as well as support groups. Amazingly, this online community became so close that even as the pandemic was ending and people were able to start attending worship in person, many did not want to give up their online community, and congregations like Am Yisrael in

Northfield offered both online and in person options.

With the racial equity challenges that were raised with the death of George Floyd in 2020, Temple Chai of Long Grove picked up on that moment by scheduling a series of workshops and speakers so members could learn more about racial equity and ways to think about their behavior and actions. These classes and talks were met with great interest and participation from congregants who enjoyed learning and growing together, even online. For both the organizers of the series of events and the congregants, it made their day to see it come off and received so successfully.

MENTAL AND EMOTIONAL SUPPORT

During the first few months of the pandemic, Morag rode the emotional rollercoaster ride that the pandemic triggered. She shared, "Throughout my life, I've carefully curated the 'British stiff upper lip' and tried hard to keep swirling emotions internalized. However, I remember one particularly dark day when one of my team called me out of the blue to check in. She asked how I was, and when I replied with a chirpy, 'fine,' she kept prodding until she got to the truth. In that moment, her compassion, her care and concern brought us together and enabled us to connect at a whole new level. Even now, as I recall that conversation a few weeks later, it still makes my day." Finding ways to connect with others beyond "I'm fine, let's go" when working virtually is so important, and even more so when each day brings a new "challenge" or "adventure." Not every conversation needs to be in depth, but some need to help us go to our gut and get it out. Thank goodness for colleagues who know this and care.

POSITIVITY AND OUTREACH ABOUNDS

Lisa says, "During the pandemic, our neighbors were painting rocks with Disney characters, messages of hope, and happy designs. It has been amazing to walk by and find one of these, left for whoever needs a pick-me-up. My daughter Emily and I joined in and now paint rocks weekly and leave them all over the neighborhood. We even left some outside of our house so we could see the joy on other kids' faces when they discover one."

What's a way to get food to those in the neediest of communities? The Love Fridge, according to *Chicago Tribune* columnist Heidi Stevens, was "the brainchild of Chicago musician Ramon Norwood, and there are more than twenty around Chicago." According to their website, "The Love Fridge is a Chicago mutual aid group grounded in food, working to place community refrigerators across the city. We are powered by kindness, generosity, love, and the belief that being able to feed yourself is a right, not a privilege. Our goal is to nourish our communities while combating food scarcity and food waste, and working with other like-minded community partners." Stevens describes a family that routinely contributed to the Love Fridge. "Annie Swingen and her husband and son have a weekly tradition: They collect coupons all week and hit the Jewel grocery store early Saturday morning. Each person gets a list and a cart to help fill the Love Fridges. After they shop, they hit different Love Fridges around the city." I love that.

These are the times that truly test our belief in making someone's day, when the stakes—life and death—are on the line. Mental illness and suicidal tendencies have doubled during the pandemic. People need help and support and are out there figuring out ways to make someone's day better to get through challenging times. There's no better time to make someone's day than during a crisis.

John Baldoni, who leads the podcast Grace Under Pressure, wrote a book during the pandemic called *Grace Notes: Leading in an Upside-Down World*. He begins the book with this poem, "Because of Covid."

"We have strength. We have resilience. We have opportunities.
We have one another.
In many ways, we've pared our lives down to what's essential.
Our loved ones, our families, our friends, and our colleagues.
Because of Covid.
While there is much to mourn, and much to fear in our current world,
There are also new learnings, new opportunities . . . Because of Covid."

PUTTING INTO PRACTICE

Showing resilience during a crisis such as the COVID-19 pandemic can make someone's day. I call it the normal now instead of the new normal because things changed so frequently. Except for kindness, generosity, caring, and compassion. Coming together during crises and helping one another make it through or recover is putting Make Someone's Day in action.

What can you do or what have you done to help others in need? Whether it's a donation, a service you can provide, a phone call or a visit, think of how you would like to help those less fortunate during challenging times. Be sure to take care of yourself in the process, too.

Can Make Someone's Day help even when people are dealing with rudeness and incivilities? You bet, as chapter ten explains.

CHAPTER 10

. . . .

OVERCOMING RUDENESS
AND INCIVILITY

"If something can be changed, work to change it. If it cannot, why worry, be upset, and complain?" —8th-century Buddhist
scholar and monk Shantideva

DO YOU GET FRUSTRATED and even angry at people who appear to be impolite or rude to you? Make Someone's Day can help here, too. Amir Erez and Christine Porath, Professors of Management at the University of Florida, researched that very topic by studying critical care doctors. They found that exposure to rudeness had a negative effect on their ability to diagnose and treat their patients. In another study, customer service reps who experienced rudeness made more errors. Whatever line of work, rudeness makes things worse, and what's more, people don't get over it. It can affect your performance and concentration all day and even longer.

Why? Rudeness is perceived as a threat, so people focus on it far longer than necessary. That detracts from whatever tasks they may need to be doing and affects performance. "There are," according to Porath and Erez, "different forms of rudeness. Rudeness that's instigated by a direct authority figure, rudeness delivered by a third party, and imagined rudeness—all converged to produce the same effects. Results from these studies showed that rudeness reduced performance on routine tasks as well as on creative tasks." People experience a decline in performance and in thinking after being treated rudely. And often it's not easy to get over quickly, and we end up dwelling on it far longer than needed.

BAD BOSSES

Work is where we spend eighty percent of our time, so if we are upset by rude people who we see regularly and interact with, it can seriously impact our productivity and even our careers. It can rob us of the desire and instinct to make someone's day because we just want to make it through our own day. My dad had two bosses. One he absolutely loved and thrived with. Every time he mentioned his name, my dad smiled and had a twinkle in his eye. He truly was a mentor for my dad. The other boss was rude and made my dad upset, angry, and frustrated. The mere thought of him made my dad cringe.

I've had many bosses in my career, some who were motivating, positive, and worked to make my day like the ones described in chapter eight. These bosses inspired me to accomplish award-winning work. I couldn't wait to go to work every day because they elevated my spirit and both supported and improved my ideas. I hope you've had some energizing bosses and, if you are a boss, choose to be that way yourself by making someone's day for your people.

Sadly, I've had many more bosses throughout my career who were rude, uninspiring, and even toxic, and my work and attitude suffered. I'm sure my health suffered as well with frequent back and stomach pain from the stress. Work became a chore I had to endure. I had less energy, and it was challenging to keep a positive outlook and think about anyone other than myself. Do you know what I mean? Sadly, throughout our careers, we have more bad bosses than not. I hope if you're a boss who wants to do the right thing, you'll learn to make someone's day and, as a result, be a boss who's memorable and admired.

Which type of bosses have you had? Have they impacted your performance? If you have to put up with a bad boss, remember that nothing is forever, and you can get through this. Whatever it takes, find what you need to get through this time and get to a better boss and place.

HAVE A BEST FRIEND AT WORK

Having a best friend at work and others you can commiserate with and help get you through the negativity and rudeness truly helped me. I also loved the work that I did which helped. Resilience is what we all need to get through the tough times. Find whatever silver lining you can in the situation, and a best friend as Morag Barrett writes about is certainly a key.

For many years, the number one reason that people leave a job is because of their manager or boss. EY's post-pandemic research in 2021 continued to confirm this top reason for leaving a job. Bamboo HR in 2020 found that forty-four percent of people leave their jobs because of a boss, not for better pay or better work elsewhere, as is too often assumed. So much is entailed in having the right people as leaders, training them in the right leadership skills, enhancing their natural instincts, providing a coach and a mentor, and then matching the right boss with the right employee. Be patient. Remember that people who are leaders may have been great practitioners first and need to grow and learn the skills of being a good leader.

FIND A WAY TO IMPROVE YOUR ATTITUDE

Attitude and your support network can make such a great difference even in challenging work atmospheres. For one stretch of time, several colleagues and I would gather in a small breakout room when we felt beat up or in despair. Our workplace was a toxic atmosphere at that time with a leader who prided himself on being a bully. Marion, Bill, Jay, and I frequently spent a moment in gratitude and prayer, thankful for being there for each other. We prayed to help us make it through the day and allow us to get our work done and inspire others. We all were of different faiths, but that didn't matter; we prayed together. Other colleagues would learn what we were doing and occasionally join us. We prayed for greater sanity around us and to hold our heads high. We succeeded. Do whatever it takes to help you outlast a terrible boss. All four of us have gone on to thrive in our careers. I hope this doesn't happen to you, but if it does, know that with the right help and support network, you too can make it through your day and overcome a rude and toxic boss. Find ways to create good, positive, practices that work for you.

Sometimes rudeness is our perception. How many times are you driving and upset by the apparent rudeness of other drivers? I was driving on the highway and trying to change lanes to exit, and a truck driver cut me off. Does that ever happen to you? I eventually changed lanes a short while later and passed him at the exit ramp. A flash of anger went through me such as motioning with a certain finger. Then I said to myself, "Just shrug it off, get rid of those negative thoughts, let them go. I'm safe, nothing happened, now let me get to where I need to go safely and forget about it." Too often, road rage occurs because we are so upset by the rudeness of others and believe it's directed at us personally. Ninety-nine point nine percent of the time, it's not directed at you. That's worth repeating. The great majority of times something happens on the road, it's not about us. The other driver doesn't even know you! Eliminate that thinking. It's simply not worth it to escalate these actions, which can lead to greater hostility and even tragic accidents. Rule 1: Don't take road rage personally. It's not about you! Rule 2: Don't engage or escalate. (I worried what would happen to my dad as he smiled at the rude driver. Fortunately, nothing.) Rule 3: Get to where you're going safely. That's what truly matters. A minute or two doesn't matter in the long run.

TECHNIQUES TO OVERCOME RUDENESS

Christine Porath says the antidote to rudeness and incivility is to thrive. In a *Harvard Business Review* article in 2016, she asks, "How can you help yourself thrive? I suggest a two-pronged approach: Take steps to thrive *cognitively,* which includes growth, momentum, and continual learning; and take steps to thrive *affectively,* by feeling healthy and experiencing passion and excitement at work and outside it. These two tactics are often mutually reinforcing—if you have energy, you're more likely to be motivated to learn, and a sense of growth fuels your vitality." Recognize which area you may need to work on so you can take steps to thrive and better withstand incivility. Fill up your life with activities that bring you passion and joy. Meditation, yoga, and exercise all help get rid of negative feelings.

When you feel rudeness from a stranger or if you've dealt with a rude boss or colleague, these experiences stay with you. Injustice in whatever form does not feel right. You need to change the message and memory. Porath shares, "Neuroscientists have shown that memories attached to strong emotions are easier to access and more likely to be replayed, and ruminating on an incident prevents you from putting it behind you. This can cause greater insecurity, lead to lower self-esteem and a heightened sense of helplessness. I encourage people to shift their focus to cognitive growth instead. Your conscious brain can think about only so many things at once—far better that it keeps busy building new neural connections and laying down new memories." Bottom line: don't let someone else's rudeness affect your life. Focus on what is important to you and spend your energy more wisely and usefully. The past is just that—it's over, it's passed. Let it go and move forward.

Christine Porath also cites sleep as particularly important to our health and mental well-being. "A lack of sleep increases your susceptibility to distraction and robs you of self-control. It makes you feel less trusting, more hostile, more aggressive, and more threatened even by weak stimuli, and can induce unethical behavior. In short, sleep deprivation (usually defined as getting less than five hours a night) is a recipe for responding poorly to incivility and perhaps even damaging to your career." Don't try to be a hero by not taking the time you need to rest and feel restored. Burning the candle doesn't provide the rest you need. Get out any anger, frustration, or sadness at the gym, kneading dough, going for a walk or bike ride, or meditating. This can also lead to better sleep. If you've had a particularly bad night, taking a short nap during the day can help restore you if your energy wanes. That's much healthier than the nearby vending machine crying out to you!

Porath states that exercise "enhances both cognitive firepower and mood, distracts you from your concerns, reduces muscle tension, and improves resilience. It has been shown to slash symptoms of anxiety by more than fifty percent. Mindfulness—shifting your consciousness to process situations more slowly and thoughtfully and to respond with greater premeditation—can help you maintain your equilibrium in a difficult environment, as can finding a sense of purpose in your job." Many books are written about the benefits of exercise, meditation, yoga, and other restorative practices. Taking care of your health has a lifetime of payoffs, including healthier longevity. Make your own day so you can have a healthier future and the ability to make someone else's.

Journaling and other rituals are other techniques that can help bring closure to the feeling of being slighted or treated rudely. David Brooks described how President Eisenhower used this process. In his book *The Road to Character*, he writes, "Dwight D. Eisenhower often wrote furious invectives in his journal to release negative emotions related to colleagues. He started the habit while working as an aide to the famously tyrannical General Douglas MacArthur." We need to get the anger or upset feeling out of our system, rather than just trying to bury or ignore it. Use journaling to get a healthy release from whatever has you upset. Don't let yourself be dragged down by comments from others or feelings of self-doubt. We all have those. Keep your focus and attitude more positive leading to greater success and happiness.

CREATING MORE KINDNESS AND HAPPINESS

Paul Mack, MD, wrote about "The Five Traits of Extraordinary Ordinary People" in *Psychology Today*. He identified five categories for real happiness and success:

1) A focus on things that matter (hint: having more is not the answer)
2) Kindness
3) A willingness to be seen as imperfect
4) An ability to connect
5) Joyfulness

Two of the five factors he cites relate directly to making someone's day: kindness and the ability to connect. The other three areas—focus on things that matter, willingness to be seen as imperfect, and joyfulness—are all areas that are in your power to do something about. In Chapter 8, I mentioned the Fish philosophy to choose your attitude. Taking care of yourself and your own emotional well-being will allow you to have more capacity to make someone's day more often.

Another way to promote healthy mental growth is to work with a mentor or coach. A mentor is someone who has a desire to help you by providing insights and knowledge they have learned along the way to overcome life's challenges, including rudeness. Mentors help you thrive and move forward toward success by being a guide and taking you under their wings while nurturing your career and life. Think of Yoda to Luke Skywalker or a polished ballplayer helping out the young rookie. What separates a mentor from the average network contact is a long-term commitment and a deep-seated investment in your future. And what's great is there is no limit on the number of mentors you can have in your life! The key is to stay in touch with them, reach out to them for specific purposes, and keep them informed of how you're doing. As someone who has mentored a number of leaders, it's very rewarding to do so.

A coach, on the other hand, can help you overcome specific challenges. Today there are coaches for many areas of life, from personal training to career/life balance to business and leadership skills. To know whether you need a coach or a mentor, think of it this way. A coach is like a private music teacher you pay to learn how to play better. That's how you can improve your skill. A mentor is like a musical veteran who provides advice on making it in the music field. What do you need right now—a coach to help you grow and overcome challenges or a mentor to get some practical advice? And since they are different, consider having both!

Positive relationships within and outside the office provide an emotional uplift that can directly counterbalance the effects of incivility. My involvement in my professional association assured me that I was getting continuous learning and development throughout my career when my workplace wasn't supportive. This involvement has led to a built-in network for mentoring, advice, and support. Whether it's through an association, club, or hobby, look for a way to continue your growth. Find the right organization for you and volunteer in ways that help you grow and that you find fulfilling. Use it as a chance to learn, grow, connect, and have fun. And remember that volunteering often gives you the chance to practice and develop your own leadership style as well as meet people with similar interests.

In college I did research on the topic of power. I wanted to know if people with formal power have more success. The short answer: no. It was the people who didn't use their power or had informal power that were the most successful. This was even true in the military, where power is clearly delineated by hierarchy and by rank. In further research, I discovered that everyone needs to feel some power someplace, whether on the softball team, serving on a committee or board, playing an instrument, or being a master chef in the kitchen. Everyone needs someplace where they can feel they are in their element. What gives you the satisfaction and opportunity to be at your best, to have a feeling of responsibility and a sense of control and centeredness?

PUTTING INTO PRACTICE

Don't let rudeness and incivility distract you from being your best. Overcome rudeness and incivility through support, through using your network, and through focusing on what Stanford professor and psychologist Carol Dweck calls a growth mindset, where you have the opportunity to grow and develop vs. a fixed mindset where you believe things cannot change. By putting your attention on growth and support, relaxation and friendship, exercise and inspiration, you give yourself the best chance to overcome rudeness and make someone's day!

What's your sweet spot, a place where you feel most comfortable? It can be in the home or office, on a committee or in a house of worship, on the ballfield or out enjoying nature. What makes you successful, joyous, or relaxed when you're there? Think about those behaviors or actions and how you can duplicate or recall that feeling at times when faced with stress or rudeness to give yourself greater confidence. Make a plan to do so now, at a time you don't feel that way, and see how it helps.

Sometimes the hardest people to show we've changed are the ones closest to us, the ones we spend the most time with throughout our lives, our families. Make Someone's Day can improve relationships with your family, too, as chapter eleven shows.

CHAPTER 11

· ·

STRENGTHENING FAMILY RELATIONSHIPS

"It's not so much what we have in life that matters. It's what we do with what we have." —Fred Rogers

WHO DO WE SEE the most throughout our lives? Our immediate and extended family. According to WebMD, "You and your family members have been doing a certain dance for decades, and everyone knows their footwork. The minute you try to change it up, you're going to step on toes. This is especially true around the holidays, when we tend to revert to our twelve-year-old selves. 'You go back to your original dynamics,' says Karen Sherman, PhD, a psychologist and relationship specialist in Long Island, New York. 'They get recreated because the family is together, and it's stressful. In times of stress, we revert to old patterns.'"

How do you show up to activities, to family gatherings, to special occasions? Frequently past history dictates who we "are" and how we are "seen." These can be challenging depending on your family dynamics, but making someone's day can make a difference. Whether it's the family we are born or adopted into, the family we gained through our spouse/partner/significant other, or the family we built through friendships, these can be some of the best and also most challenging relationships. If you can improve these relationships and the dialogue by making someone's day, you can look forward to these events in a better light. It can change the dynamics of your relationships with those closest to you and who you see the most.

CHANGE THE NARRATIVE

The hardest part about family is that even as we grow older, we are often thought about as to how we were in the past, and we often think of others in the same way. Who calls you Billy, Howie, or Barbie today except for people who have known you most of your life? And sometimes because of that, family members revert back to thinking of your past behavior as well. How do you get around that? Change the narrative! You're not the same person today as you were growing up, and neither are they.

Carrie Sloan from WebMD elaborates further. "The thing about family dynamics is that they're very resilient," says Guy Winch, PhD, a psychologist in private practice and the author of *Emotional First Aid*. "When one person tries to change their role, the family will try to snap them back into it. There's an active resistance." Say you have a "bad" sibling who gets all the attention, while you never feel heard. "Your family is used to organizing around that theme," explains Winch. And you usually have a part in it. "After all those years, you're not going to speak up about things that are going on with you," he says. "We become complicit with the dynamics even in ways we're not aware—or fond—of."

Sloan suggests two ways to revise an unwanted role:

1) "Watch for familiar cues. One common dynamic Winch sees is tension between parents and adult kids who tiptoe home for the holidays. For example, maybe you're so used to your parents' bickering that you hesitate to start a real conversation because you're already braced for them to start arguing.

2) "Ask yourself, 'If I were in a different environment, how would I be behaving?' Then behave that way. 'If you were at a friend's house, what would you be talking about?' says Winch. 'It might not be

comfortable to go into your parents' house when you're waiting for a fight to erupt and say, "Guess what happened to me on the plane?" But you should.'"

CHANGE WHAT'S IN YOUR CONTROL

If others think you're always late, surprise them by being early or on time, and when you do, don't be upset at them if they're late. Just keep up the new behavior. If you're not one to praise your siblings or parents, change your tune and do so. Find ways to compliment your family members and be proud of what they do and most care about—that in itself may make their day.

What else can you do? Control what you can, and let go of what you can't control. Do you always insist on the restaurant or place to go to? Don't. And if they always make the choices, let them. What if you're not happy with their choice? Offer suggestions and alternatives and a reason why—someplace is too noisy, too crowded, doesn't have what you can eat now, etc. Or just let it go. It's one time, one meal. Your agreement to their choice may make life better for you and for them and be the change that causes them to see you differently.

IS IT WORTH IT?

Changing the dialogue of the voices in our heads and theirs isn't easy. It may take time to turn off the tapes from the past and start a new recording. The difference with family is you know what they may be asking, thinking, and saying—you already know their V(iew) from the VIP Model and how they like to be recognized. Use that information!

Ask yourself is it worth it? Chances are since you will see your family your whole life, it is definitely worth it. Here's more advice from Carrie Sloan of WebMD. "Resisting your usual family dynamic is going to create fallout. 'It's going to feel funny,' says Guy Winch. 'It can feel tense, uncomfortable, even unsafe. Those are all [common] responses when you're changing behavior.' Truth be told, your family pattern may not change right away, even if you radically revise your own behavior. But keep at it. While you may not be able to change your family, you can definitely change yourself and control your own reaction to them. And that's a positive change in itself."

BE GENEROUS WITH COMPLIMENTS

One of the biggest and easiest ways to change the dialogue is with a compliment, a good word, a positive affirmation. Be free and generous with those. When I had tuba lessons with the late, great Arnold Jacobs of the Chicago Symphony, he always said, "Take as big a breath as you can. The air is free!" Same thing with compliments—give them freely and frequently, especially when they're not expected. Be specific and genuine with your compliments. "That shirt looks really good on you!" "So glad you were able to get together today." "Thanks for making the time!" It doesn't cost you anything and can make a difference toward a family member who didn't think you noticed or that you cared what they were wearing, what they said, or what they cared about. Do so now. Don't wait. Rebuilding and renewing these dynamics in a new way can be freeing.

There are more ways to change past dialogue. If you always argue or disagree, don't. Just don't get into it. Make someone's day by avoiding the issue? Why not! It shows that you've grown, that getting along is more important than being "right" or having the last word. It's a new side of you, that you are different and that you want to create new memories together. The only time to bring up painful past memories is if you can both laugh at them now. Use humor to let them go. Consider making fun of yourself or your earlier actions, which allows others to gently tease you and not hammer you about them. Because when you grow up together, you know each other's hot spots.

LET IT GO

A lot of this is easier said than done. When you put long-held beliefs and family dynamics together, it can bring up old feelings of frustration, anger, and even distrust. Try to minimize those feelings and contain them. It doesn't do anyone any good to hang onto the past. As my mentor Marshall Goldsmith and the song from *Frozen* says, let it go. It's not worth it. We need to shed those arguments that want to stay with us. Let them go.

According to a 2012 study by AARP, there is a hunger to improve family relationships by improving relationships with parents first, spouse/partner second, and siblings third. There's a TV show called *Blue Bloods* that's about both NYPD and interfamily relationships. On the show, there are three generations of family members in law enforcement. They all gather together weekly for a large family dinner, typically at the end of the show. The dynamics are out there for all to see, yet like most TV dramas, they resolve themselves within the hour. Each person gets a chance to say what's on their minds. Then the patriarch has them listening to and supporting each other, and eventually they all get there.

You may have to do this in small steps. That's okay—this is family, and you are guaranteed to see them throughout your life. They may think you're nuts. That's okay—they're family, and they probably are a little cuckoo, too. Why not show them a better selection of nuts? Ones that are more tolerant, more giving, more caring, and more appreciative.

Staying more frequently in touch with family may be all that's needed. When I was growing up, we used to call my grandmother in New York every Sunday morning. Those calls were heaven for my sister and myself and truly a lifeline for our nana. Anything that brought us closer to her—even just hearing her voice—was good. Being her only grandchildren, I'm sure she felt the same way when hearing our voices. Today with video social media and apps such as FaceTime, Skype, and Zoom, those moments are all the more powerful than just a phone call. If you want to keep your family connected and make their day, make sure your grandparents, aunts, and uncles have a way of connecting with you that allows you to show up and see them on a more regular basis, in person or electronically. More frequent connections may make the big get-togethers easier to take and will strengthen the new impression you are trying to achieve.

SHARE ADVENTURES AND SOAK UP THEIR KNOWLEDGE

My dad passed away over thirty years ago, and my mom has remained a widow. My sister and I each try to do activities with her we think she would enjoy. I've taken her on trips (remember she's a travel agent and loves travel) and play concerts at her senior home. My sister takes her to the theater frequently, especially musicals, something my mother loves, and has also travelled with her. Does it matter to our mom at this point? We aren't sure, as she has dementia. But is she happy? Yes. That's what counts. And the best thing? We each get to spend time with her doing things she enjoys and we each enjoy as well. We work to make her day every day and every time we see her.

What are you most thankful for from your parents? What did they teach you? Do they know the impact they had on your life? Besides teaching me about sports, Mom got me interested in international friendships through being a pen pal in third grade, and that contributed to my desire for travel and making friends around the world. She took me to folk concerts and folk dancing. I have these and so many more hobbies now to be thankful for from her. And Dad taught me many lessons about how to treat others well and the value of preparation, hard work, and love of extended family.

What about your siblings, grandparents, aunts, uncles, cousins? They all contributed to making you who you are. And they care about you. Try to thank them as well and show them the new you through a phone call, a note, a shared memory, a story, or a poem. My wife's father would cancel any plans if a family event was happening, even if it was a last-minute dinner invitation. He always said family came first and lived by that rule.

DO IT NOW—NO REGRETS

Do you have close friends who feel like family? My friend Ron lives on the East Coast, and I learned he had prostate cancer and was going to have surgery. I checked in with him every week to hear the latest medical report and how he's feeling. Even when we can't talk, I love to at least hear his voice on his voicemail and leave him a message. Am I making his day? I don't know—often we don't know—but I hope the check-ins provide some comfort as well as the knowledge of how much I do care about him and his health.

CREATING NEW TRADITIONS

As your family grows or moves, create new family traditions that can be a part of who you are. Elizabeth writes about a new family tradition she started: "Creating new Thanksgiving traditions, my family does not hold back. Morning brunch, afternoon disc golf, folding napkins into turkeys around the dinner table, we love our annual traditions." And she's always open to trying something new. For example, one Thanksgiving, people were writing notes to family members and friends around the table and telling them what they appreciate about them. These could be funny, caring, sad, silly or just memorable moments. Through tears and laughter, these became a special part of her Thanksgiving tradition and made the day of everyone who participated.

Our family is who we have. We can either bemoan them or celebrate them. We can either gripe about them or hype about them. Make their day and yours by taking the road less travelled and celebrate the best of who they are and who you are.

PUTTING INTO PRACTICE

The people we have known the longest are our family. We have dynamics that go back to growing up and sometimes create angst in gatherings. Change your dialogue and expectations. Show them a new side of you by making their day. Instead of tiptoeing on eggshells, create new and positive dynamics and traditions. It's never too late.

Who in your life do you want to change the dynamics with? Identify that person and one thing you will do differently. How does that feel, even to think about? If it feels okay, what else can you do (or not do)? Make a plan to start as soon as you can and replace the tapes in your heads.

In chapter twelve, we'll look at giving thanks to those who made your life, with many unforgettable moments.

CHAPTER 12

GIVING THANKS TO PEOPLE
WHO MADE YOUR LIFE

"It's not enough to have lived. We should be determined to live for something. May I suggest that it be creating joy for others, sharing what we have for the betterment of person-kind, bringing hope to the lost and love to the lonely."
—Leo Buscaglia

WHO HAS IMPACTED YOU and played an important role in your life? Would you like an opportunity to properly thank them, even years later? Throughout our lives, different people impact us, hopefully more positively than negatively. Besides bosses, these can include teachers, colleagues, customers, mentors, and others who believed in us and who helped us along the way. The earliest people who fit that description are your teachers, parents, siblings, and friends.

YOUR FORMER TEACHERS AND COACHES WANT TO HEAR FROM YOU

Reunions should give you a chance to thank teachers as well as catch up with former classmates. I recently did that. I was a music geek in high school and played tuba in a number of ensembles. The people I played with crossed all the years in school, from seniors my freshman year to freshmen my senior year. On my high school reunion weekend every five years, I organize a music reunion for all music alumni, whatever year they graduated. The last time we did this, Mr. Owens, our retired band director, came out to join and greet us. A number of the people there had gone on to have illustrious musical careers, all of whom were influenced by him. On behalf of all of us, I thanked him for his tremendous musical knowledge, inspiration, and support. He was embarrassed and pleased by the comments and to see so many of his former students. You can do that, too—it's never too late to thank someone who made your day or life!

How did I get hooked on music? Dr. Herbert Zipper, a Holocaust survivor, brought his orchestra to grade schools in Evanston, Illinois, where I grew up. That in itself is a story that became an Oscar-nominated documentary, *Never Give Up: The 20th Century Odyssey of Herbert Zipper*. He was also a subject in many papers, including the *New York Times*, which wrote, "As an inmate at Dachau concentration camp in the late 1930s, Dr. Zipper arranged to have crude musical instruments constructed out of stolen material and formed a small secret orchestra which performed on Sunday afternoons for the other inmates. Together with a friend, he composed the 'Dachau Lied' ('Dachau Song'), which was learned by the other inmates. Released in 1939, he accepted an invitation to conduct the Manila Symphony Orchestra. Jailed for four months by the Japanese during their occupation of the Philippines, after his release, he worked secretly for the Allies, transmitting shipping information by radio. After the war, he emigrated to the United States in 1946, where he conducted the Brooklyn Symphony Orchestra and promoted music education." He came to the Chicago area, where he performed for thousands of children in Evanston and other Chicago-area schools who would come and listen to his annual young people concerts. I was fascinated with the concerts and what I learned about music from listening to his explanation and selections, which spurred my desire to play in a band or orchestra.

In fifth grade, I was part of the All-City Choir and was asked to play the bells for one number. (Obviously after hearing me sing, my music teacher realized my talents deserved to be heard differently than singing.) The opportunity to play bells in All-City was exciting and furthered my desire to be in the junior high band. This is an example of people who made my day early on—an orchestra and a conductor, a music teacher, and a band director, Mr. Barrett, who encouraged me to play tuba in sixth grade. I have never put it down, still playing fifty years later, and continue to perform in several bands and groups. Music, and tuba, has made my life. And I had a chance to thank several of my band directors later as an adult.

Another example also from fifth grade, obviously a pivotal year in my life, was when I went to visit a Boy Scout Troop as I was crossing over from Cub Scouts. The Troop I visited took a break in meetings so kids could let off some energy. This evening they were playing a game called bombardment, which involved two teams across the room from each other with several volleyballs. The balls were thrown at the other team. If the ball hit you, you were out. If you caught it, they were out. I was one of the smallest and youngest there and caught the ball of someone much older. I think when it was thrown at me, I just hung on for dear life! Everyone cheered me on. It made me feel welcomed and confirmed that this was the Troop I wanted to be a part of, one where younger Scouts would feel welcomed by older ones. I continue to volunteer in Scouting and love how older Scouts help and support younger ones while they develop their own leadership and team skills. This lifetime of commitment to Scouting was based on something that happened very spontaneously and made my day when I was eleven years old. As a result, I started a Scout Troop for my son Jordan when he turned eleven, and I became his Scoutmaster. And my original Scoutmaster, Mr. Gibson, became my son's first leader at camp. I was both able to thank him for what he taught me and have him teach my son. These experiences can transform who we are and are unforgettable, even forty-five years later. I attribute my time as a youth in Scouting to leading me to my career in learning and development because I loved the emphasis Scouting places on teaching leadership and team skills.

I can imagine other teachers wondering if they made a lasting difference in their students' lives. It would be great to let them know that. I've been amazed that some of these teachers remember me all these years later and am fortunate to have thanked some of them for what they taught me and how their lessons stay with me. I've also had the reverse happen. I saw a teacher at a concert I was playing who thanked me for being in his class! We had a nice chat after the concert. This made me think, "What did I do that made a difference for him?" Can you imagine being thanked by a teacher you had years later? Someone who made a difference in your life was also touched by you. Thank you, Larry Olson, for coming up to me, saying hello, and telling me this. You made my day when you did.

I fondly remember the teachers that opened my eyes to so many areas and gave me skills, insight, values, and a critical thinking process that has guided me throughout my life. I was invited to the retirement party of one teacher who was very influential in my appreciation and understanding of the non-western world. All of us, whatever year we had Owen Hein for English and history, felt the same way (which was amazing to me that he influenced so many in the same way that he influenced me). We were all able to tell him how much his teaching impacted our lives.

I had breakfast with my college guidance counselor not too long ago. Chuck helped me choose a college major, determine if I should transfer schools, and decide about graduate school. Talk about being there at pivotal moments of my life! What about you—what teachers and leaders helped you? Have you had a chance to reconnect with them? Have lunch with people who impacted your life. They'll appreciate it, and you'll be making their day, after they did such a great job making yours!

Arlene tells the story about getting a note years later from a former accounting student as to how she made his life. He went on to get a degree in accounting and have a successful career. And it was all because of her accounting class and how she inspired him. As a teacher, that's as good as it gets. It's what you hope happens, but you rarely know, unless someone reaches out to tell you. Reach out now and make the day of a former teacher by letting them know how they made your day and life. It's never too late.

When you dedicate yourself to teaching, mentoring, or coaching, you never know who will benefit the most or how they benefit from the way you've helped them. You do the best you can for everyone. Many times students and others don't say anything to you, but you know you have influenced them and contributed to their future lives and success. For example, colleagues in my profession have told me how much I inspired them in their careers and encouraged them. It's very rewarding to hear that. To me, seeing them succeed was enough of a reward. Yet years later when they thanked me, that felt great and made my day. Have you influenced and mentored others, too? Did other kids, young adults, and new workers look up to you? Did you coach any sports or volunteer with your child as a youth leader? It's a great feeling to help others, get involved, and be a role model, and I heartily recommend it. I don't have any idea as to how many people's lives I touched or impacted. I don't think anyone in teaching, leadership, or social services does, nor do volunteer leaders, coaches, or tutors. Seeing others learn, grow, and succeed is why we do it.

THANK OTHER ADULTS WHO INFLUENCED YOU

Take a moment to think of all the adults and leaders who influenced you as a youth. Consider how they've contributed to who you are by providing knowledge, guidance, and inspiration in school and extracurricular activities such as sports, religious school, scouts, music, art, dance, etc. At the time, all they needed was to see us grow through listening, learning, hard work, and cooperating at whatever activity you were doing. What did that class or activity lead to—a career, a lifetime hobby, or lifelong friends? Insights and passion for an activity? Were you the one that your teacher was excited about and who made a difference in your life? Thank them!

What about your parents? If your parents were supportive of you, how can you ever properly thank them? I was fortunate to be able to do so for my mom, as my dad passed away many years ago and I hope he knew how I felt about him. I was asked to contribute a story to a book, *Leadership Lessons for Any Occasion: Stories from Our Mothers* by Ed and Nila Betof, and share the impact Mom had on me as a leader. I was delighted to write about how "Mom Taught Me the Score." Mom was a big sports fan, both watching and listening to baseball (Chicago Cubs), and actively playing tennis and bowling every week. She took me to baseball games and taught me about the game she loved and how to keep score, much like her uncles had taught her in New York. My love of baseball is from her. She was a sportswriter in the 1940s, and my life has given me that opportunity to be a sports columnist for two Florida papers today. Her involvement in bowling influenced me to start my own bowling league in fifth grade, and she taught me how to keep score in bowling, too. On Mother's Day after the book was published, I gave her a copy and read her my story about how she taught me the score. She was pleased. Too often we think about doing these things after the fact. It's never too late to say something or write something to the people you care about. Share the remembrance at a holiday or family gathering or just give it to them. Take the time now and do it in a way that works for you.

THANKING THOSE WHO BELIEVED IN YOU

What happens when life isn't so easy? Sometimes people take a wrong turn and are lucky to stumble into something that is not just life changing, it can be lifesaving. The Jesse White Tumblers in Illinois just celebrated sixty years of taking youth from the toughest neighborhoods in Chicago and showing them a different future with jumping and tumbling. Over ten thousand youth have been a part of the Jesse White Tumblers over those sixty years, and all stayed clear of drugs, gangs, and violence. That was part of their agreement to stay with the tumblers. Here's what Jesse White himself had to say: *"I believe that when you go through this world and become successful, you should give something back. I also believe that you should do something good for someone every day."* Thank you, Jesse White, Illinois Secretary of State and lifelong public official, for your lifetime of commitment to our youth.

Frances Hesselbein still receives notes every year from the girls she shepherded as a Girl Scout leader. They stay in touch and remind her what a difference she made in their lives. Frances became an "accidental" scout leader because no one else agreed to do it, even though she didn't have a daughter. In the seventies, she was the first head of the Girl Scouts of the USA who came up through the ranks from a youth leader. Frances literally righted the boat when things were shaky for them. For all her work leading the Girl Scouts, leading the Peter Drucker Foundation, and so much more, Frances was awarded the Presidential Medal of Freedom. Frances continues to work every day in her hundreds, making a difference for others and inspiring many. Her favorite saying is from George Bernard Shaw: "I am of the opinion that my life belongs to the community, and as long as I live, it is my privilege to do whatever I can. I want to be thoroughly used up when I die, for the harder I work, the more I live. Life is no 'brief candle' to me. It is a sort of splendid torch which I have got hold of for a moment, and I want to make it burn as brightly as possible before handing it on to the future generations." Frances is always making someone's day.

One more Scout story, this one about homeless girls in Queens. Talk about a desperate need and time to make someone's life. Giselle Burgess is a single mom with five children who works for the Girl Scouts of Greater New York as a community development specialist. Her apartment building closed, and she couldn't find a place that would accept her and her children on her salary and ended up living in a hotel for homeless people. She had one room and two beds for the six of them. In her job, she helped start new troops and recruited new Girl Scouts. Burgess asked if she could start a troop in her shelter, and the response was an enthusiastic yes. All twenty-eight of the girls in Troop 6000 live at the hotel. They're members of the first-ever Girl Scout troop for girls who are homeless. "I try to stress the fact that they are just like any other Girl Scout troop," says Burgess, who started Troop 6000 in February 2017. "The only difference between us is at the end of our meetings we are still in the same location. When people think about homelessness, they think about the man on the corner who came from out of state and has the cardboard sign. I think my biggest goal is to try to break that stigma of homelessness." The troop, which includes three of Burgess' daughters, does the same work as other Girl Scout troops, practicing first aid, learning about STEM careers, earning badges, and selling cookies. The program has been so successful that the New York City government invested $1.1 million to expand Troop 6000 from the twenty-eight girls at one shelter to as many as five hundred girls at fifteen shelters across the five boroughs of the city.

Burgess is still living at the homeless shelter. "I used to worry a lot in the beginning," Burgess says. "I became depressed and upset, [until] I began to look at it as it's not my time to leave the shelter yet. As long as I'm at the shelter, I want all the girls to keep learning. Some of the things they learn will go toward merit badges. Other things they learn will go towards life skills." Burgess hopes the scouting experience, and her own example, can teach Troop 6000 that hard times "are just seasons in their lives. And that they will surpass it, and that there's much more out there that they're capable of accomplishing." I hope that every one of these girls goes on to have great lives and lets Burgess know the impact she had on them.

PUTTING INTO PRACTICE

It's never too late to thank your parents, older adults, teachers, coaches, and leaders who made your life by what they taught you. These memories last a lifetime—don't forget them by making their day.

What experiences did you have as a youth that stand out and perhaps led you in the direction of a vocation or hobby or even your career? Did you find an experience early in life that you have kept with and became a part of who you are? What was one lesson you learned from your parents or guardian? How has that withstood the test of time and perhaps led you in the direction of a vocation or hobby or even your career? What bosses made your day? In whatever way, a card or note or better yet in person, stop and do that now or make arrangements to do so!

Now comes the fun. Chapter thirteen shares examples of best birthdays and celebrations—all of which made someone's day.

CHAPTER 13

· ·

MAKE IT FUN

"Those who are happiest are those who do the most for others."
—Booker T. Washington

MAKING SOMEONE'S DAY SHOULD be fun. And when the goal is specifically fun, you can create special occasions, celebrations, and events that make people's lives. You may think that those don't count—we were celebrating the birthday or occasion anyway. Effort put in does make a difference. Read on for some unforgettable celebrations—from simple to the extraordinary—that create memories that last a lifetime. All were exceptional for the person(s) being honored. As you read these stories and examples, think about what you might do to celebrate those you care most about.

CELEBRATIONS AT THE MOST IMPORTANT OF TIMES

Connie works at a local public library. Every day, Connie sees Phyllis, a woman in her late seventies, a "bag lady," come into the library and put her "stuff" down on a table where she sits for most of the day. Connie knows that Phyllis lives alone, doesn't have any friends, has had a hard life, and is not well off. To the rest of the library staff, she is just a crotchety old lady and nuisance who seems bitter and unpleasant. To Connie, Phyllis is someone who desperately needed someone to make her day. Connie found out that Phyllis's eightieth birthday was coming up and wanted to see if she could connect with her by providing a little dignity and celebration. Connie organized a surprise birthday party for her with the library staff. The staff was not on board at first. They wondered why they reserved a room, ordered a cake, and even reluctantly pitched in to get some presents for her. She was a thorn in their side. Connie's hope was this was just what Phyllis needed—some attention—but she wasn't sure how she would take it. Everyone was very cautious and skeptical going into it. On her birthday, Phyllis came into the library like she usually did at ten a.m. and after some reluctance and obstinacy agreed to go with Connie to a conference room. Surprise! Phyllis couldn't have been more surprised and, shockingly, thrilled. The act of noticing her, recognizing her, and celebrating her didn't just make her day—it made her year, and maybe her life. Connie thinks that Phyllis never had a birthday party, at least as an adult. The cost to Connie? Some time, money, effort, and coordination. And most importantly, the belief that everyone has a story in life and just needs to be given some attention. She felt that this was a way to get to Phyllis' heart, to preserve her humanity. And it worked out! The decorations, cake, presents, and attention was all she could ever ask for. Phyllis was a totally different person afterward, coming into the library with a smile. And the staff now had a newfound appreciation of Phyllis. Thanks to Connie for believing that all of us have humanity inside just waiting to come out, even Phyllis. Connie was thrilled it worked out so well and keeps photos of that event on her phone to remind her not to prejudge others. Here are some other best birthdays and celebrations.

Celeste was a powerhouse executive director and organizer and social worker. She impacted her community in Chicago with all of her engagement and effort to make lives better and safer and was a mother of three children under twelve. Celeste was diagnosed with breast cancer, went through treatment, seemed to be recovering, yet a year later it came back far worse than before. Her friends knew Celeste needed to be celebrated, not knowing what her future prognosis would be. With the help of the neighborhood YMCA, they planned a dance party with over two hundred guests. Celeste was surprised and thrilled. Even in her weakened state, she was out on the dance floor the whole time. It was a beautiful celebration of who she was as a person, beloved by so many in the community. Several months later, the cancer took her life. But the memory her family and friends have is a wonderful evening celebration of good food, family, and friends, something they can always look back on fondly as they remember Celeste.

The Make-A-Wish Foundation provides celebrations for people with terminal and severe illnesses. Parker was a young teen who had a rare autoimmune disease. He missed most of his middle school, taking lessons from home when he could. Fortunately, he was chosen by Make-A-Wish to receive his dream: a chance to "sign and play" with his favorite team, the Chicago Bulls, since Parker's mother and uncles grew up in Chicago. Make-A-Wish flew him up from Miami, and the Bulls "signed" him to a one-day contract. He then had a "workout" with the Bulls players, posing for many pictures and autographs. Joakim Noah was particularly caring and gave him his email and phone number. Parker has a memory for life. Thankfully, the disease is now in remission, so hopefully Parker is over the worst of it and can enjoy his life and his memories when Make-A-Wish made his day.

MEMORABLE BIRTHDAYS

Scott spent his "dream fiftieth birthday" in Paris on the Champs-Élysées in the shadow of the Arc de Triomphe, with his family watching the finale of the Tour de France. After Lance Armstrong finished his domination of the race, they walked down the boulevard to the Louvre, where they saw so much great art and especially the Mona Lisa. "This lifetime memory is forever etched in my mind and definitely made my day." We all need a remarkable birthday sometime in our lives. If need be, we can do it for ourselves.

Sharon did just that. Her favorite birthday is one she gave herself. "One of my best birthdays was my thirtieth. Since I wasn't married, I decided it was time to have a big party and invite all of my friends and relatives similar to who I'd invite to a wedding. I rented a pavilion at a park, hired a DJ, my dad and boss grilled hamburgers and hotdogs, I put my face on Budweiser stand-up displays and had them around the pavilion, we had a pinata . . . oh my goodness, it was SUCH a fun day!! To this day, twenty-five years later, it not only made my day but some people tell me it was the best birthday party they ever attended and it made their day too!! Great fun!!" Sharon, by making your day, you brought great memories to many others.

Laura's best birthday was also her thirtieth. "We planned to have a family dinner at Italian Kitchen, our favorite pizza joint in town. My twin brother picked me up, and we walked into a complete surprise party for us both! My mom had contacted all our friends and family and rented out the back room. My sister made the centerpieces from old pictures of us growing up, and they even got a palm reader for entertainment! It remained one of my favorite memories of my mother until she passed away in 2018." Sounds like this made Laura's day, her mom's day, and a lifetime of fond memories.

Barbara says it doesn't take a crowd for her best birthday. "On my fortieth birthday, my mom and dad and both siblings and their spouses came to our house in Virginia for the weekend. We had the event outside on the deck, and the best part was I had it catered so we could enjoy ourselves. Even simple things like a group bike ride were super. The weekend was so much fun. I think most birthdays are spectacular, but this one I remember fondly, and just being together made my day!!"

Theresa's friend made her birthday special. "I have a friend who knows all about board games. I told him about a game I remembered from when I was a kid. He argued that it didn't exist. Afterward he went and researched and found that it did. He bid to get a bunch of the games on eBay over several weeks to make sure he got all the pieces and gave it to me as a gift. The game was actually an awful game, but his thoughtfulness and actions were unforgettable and made my day." It's that thoughtfulness and above and beyond effort that takes something to an extraordinary and unforgettable level.

Karen shares a made my day moment when she and her husband Pat, both band directors, took their first job far away from family and friends. "My favorite birthday memory was in 1977, in Thompson Falls, Montana. I was playing the flute in my husband Pat's pep band at his school. I played the next song in the book, but the rest of the band played 'Happy Birthday' for me! I'll never forget my surprise and how they made my day." From simple to planned, from doing it yourself to being surprised, Make Someone's Day celebrations truly last a lifetime. So do proposals.

SPECIAL PROPOSALS AND LOVE STORIES

Sharon's boyfriend Mark invited her for a walk at a nature center where they had gone on their second date. His daughter Bri was with him. Suddenly, Bri drifted off. Mark then pulled Sharon toward him and said, "Sharon, this is where we started our journey together, and now I'm asking you to continue our journey as my wife." He then pulled out a ring box. Sharon was totally surprised! They had talked about the concept of getting engaged, but she didn't realize at first it was happening. She opened the ring box, and there was a picture of a ring folded into a triangle type shape to emulate the ring. Now she was confused. Sharon looked at him and asked, "Where is the ring?" Being a true accountant, he said, "Well, I wasn't sure you would say yes, so I didn't want to buy the ring just yet." Sharon started laughing, slid the paper "ring" on her finger, and said yes. She didn't think the ring would be in until a couple months later. One week later, they were having lunch with her dad, and Mark asked him for Sharon's hand in marriage. Her dad said, "Well, you know Sharon, she's going to do what she wants. If she's happy, then I'm happy." During that time, Mark placed a box in front of Sharon. Confused, she opened it, and there was the real ring to her surprise and delight! She said yes all over again! Mark made her life.

A groom-to-be from Brooklyn surprised his girlfriend by including her students at school in on the secret of his proposal after notifying their parents. The students each joined in the surprise by making decorations and each holding up a flower when he came to see her in the classroom and propose at the end of the school day. The principal and staff were in on it as well, and it made for quite the exciting buzz in the teacher's lounge at school and a most memorable proposal.

One of the most memorable moments of the Passover Seder meal is when the four questions (and answers) are recited. These questions are usually asked by the youngest person present and have been recited throughout thousands of years of Jewish history. This time I added a fifth question. I went over to my girlfriend and in front of our families asked her a fifth question: "Will you marry me?" I got an immediate yes and the delight in knowing so many people we loved were there to share in it.

Rebecca is impossible to surprise and is very analytical. "I knew she would appreciate some kind of thought-provoking proposal, so I set up a ring scavenger hunt that took her across several state lines," explains Jason. "She didn't know she was playing for marriage or a ring. She just thought we were out for a super fun and wacky Sunday afternoon because we're that kind of couple. I left clues on the bathroom mirror that led to a local brunch spot and had wait staff leave clues with her coffee. Those led her to the next spot, a park several miles away where we first met. She kept going through the trail, eighteen destinations in all, and by the end of the day, she was exhausted, out of gas, somewhat annoyed, and at her mom's house—where I proposed in front of her entire family. She likes to say now that I was preparing her for an exhausting but thoughtful marriage. Probably true."

When Marcus proposed to Jessie, he thought he planned the most perfect, dimly lit sunset dinner on the dock of a local lake in their Michigan hometown. He set up a cafe-style table, two fabric-covered chairs, brought a picnic basket, and even hired a guitar player to strum softly—what he didn't plan was the weak wooden boards at the end of the dock where he would end up kneeling to propose. By the time he was about to propose, one of the wooden boards came loose, and Jessie was tossed into the lake.

"Luckily, it was July, really warm, and I was obsessed with Marcus, so I would've said yes no matter what, but falling in definitely made it one of the most outrageous proposals we've ever even heard of," Jessie shared. They talk about falling in love, and in this case literally falling!

In the early nineties, Lori felt she was one of the few women dating on the internet, as this was relatively new. "I enjoyed dating the men whom I met there, almost all of whom were IT people because they were comfortable meeting online. This guy named Marc posted a very poetic singles ad, he signed his name, so I got his number and called him. We had a lovely conversation and agreed to meet. Later on, he told me that he was so excited that a woman had called him three hours after he posted his ad. He thought, 'I'm going to get thousands of responses!' But it was just me. In retrospect, maybe the phrase 'a man of modest means' was inadvisable. We printed his singles ad in our wedding program, and that ad—and Marc—continues to make my life."

My wife Laurie is an accountant. We decided to get married over New Year's and have our wedding on New Year's Eve, and she realized that for tax purposes it would be better to get married in the upcoming year (January 1) than the past year (December 31). What to do since we didn't want the party to start at one a.m.? We decided to have the party first, a "pre-ception" before instead of a reception afterward. After the midnight countdown, everyone went into the sanctuary for the wedding ceremony. There's only one problem. Now friends ask us every New Year if it's time for us to have another New Year's Eve anniversary party!

Mary Ann shares a most touching story of her parents' love for one another to the very end. "My parents met at Union Station in Chicago before my father went into the Army and to Korea. My mother was there with her family to see her older brother off while my father stood there at the station all alone. Not wanting him to leave without having anyone to see him off, she stood by his side until he boarded the train. They wrote letters and fell in love despite only seeing each other just a few times when he got back. My mother struggled with dementia toward the end of her life. One night as we cared for her, my father sat on a chair beside her bed, held her hand, and pulled out a journal that she had written during their trip to Israel. With tears streaming down my face, I saw the true depth of a man's love for his beautiful bride. After reading each day's account, he'd ask, 'Do you remember seeing Masada? Do you remember walking the Via Dolorosa?' I remember every detail that night listening to my father read the memories my mother had written years before. Wiping the tears from my face, I will never forget seeing the most beautiful love story first hand as he tried to make her day. He made mine."

HUMOR HELPS

Why does work and life have to be so serious? An extension of smiling is laughter, which has many health benefits, too. Jokes and humor help lighten life. My parents were great humorous storytellers. I like to use puns to bring a smile (and groan) to a conversation. Others, like my brother-in-law Phil, like to use noises and sound effects.

If a routine gets in the way of making life fun, why not break that routine? Look at how in chapter eight I described the Pike Place Fish Market in Seattle. They broke the routine of just wrapping up the fish customers selected and created the Fish philosophy with fun as a key element.

Why do late night comedians have monologues? In order for people to unwind from their day with a laugh and a smile. Humor helps.

According to *Forbes* magazine, even CEOs can benefit from learning what they can from late-night talk show hosts. A 2018 *Forbes* article is titled "Ten Reasons Why Humor is a Key to Success at Work." A Robert Half International survey found that ninety-one percent of executives believe a sense of humor is important for career advancement while eighty-four percent feel that people with a good sense of humor do a better job. Another study by Bell Leadership Institute found that the two most desirable traits in leaders were a strong work ethic and a good sense of humor. Michael Kerr, President of Humor at Work, says, "At an organizational level, some organizations are tapping into what I'd call 'the humor advantage.' Companies such as Zappos and Southwest Airlines use humor and a positive and fun culture to help brand their business, retain employees, and to attract and keep customers."

Laughter is a natural part of life. Infants begin smiling during the first weeks of life and laugh out loud within months of being born. Even if you did not grow up in a household where laughter was a common sound, you can learn to laugh anytime. Find ways to plan for humor in your day and your life. Here are some ways to start from Help Guide online.

- **Smile.** Throughout this book, smiling keeps appearing. It's also the precursor to laughter. When you start smiling more at others, they start smiling and sometimes laughing.

- **Identify what's positive in your life.** Move away from negative or worrisome thoughts—they don't add value or help you. When you're down, start thinking and counting what's going well and what you feel good about. Find a reason to smile and laugh.

- **Join the laughter.** Spend time with fun people, storytellers, and those you enjoy being with. These people are often great observers of life and make us all feel more comfortable and bring their insights into both the ordinary and ridiculous. Both my parents were great storytellers and enjoyed making a short story long to draw out the most from it. The next time you're with a group or at a party, move toward the group smiling and laughing.

- **Observe life.** Most comedians' jokes come from observation of everyday life. Seeing the absurdities in life brings us together. It's the way they interpret or talk about life that causes us to laugh. Lots of the jokes and pictures I see online are just funny observations of life, e.g. how people initially created their own face mask by wearing plastic bags and paper bags over their heads. Find humor in the ordinary and you'll be able to not take life too seriously.

Whenever I teach a class or give a talk, I try to add some fun. It might be a story or anecdote, activity or analogy, but what it does is it relaxes the group, and when that happens, it relaxes me. When I'm more relaxed,

I'm at my best, and when my participants are relaxed, they share more and are not as tense.

ATHLETES CAN CREATE SPECIAL MEMORIES IN THE COMMUNITY

Being lucky counts and can lead to a great memory like Jan's. "I played radio contests for years. One of my favorite contests involved beating three different people before I won the grand prize. The grand prize was round-trip tickets to Chicago, a stay at a hotel on Rush Street, a rental car, and two tickets to the All-Star Game at Wrigley Field. And if that's not enough, the seats were close to Lou Brock and Davey Concepcion. It was one of my favorite trips and has provided me with a lifetime memory I'll never forget."

Many athletes do a wonderful job of community service when they visit ill patients in the hospital. One of those was a Chicago Cubs outfielder, Matt Szczur, who visited Lois while she was fighting cancer. Although Lois wasn't a Cubs fan, she immediately became one because of his visit, wishes, and the Cubs paraphernalia that he gave her. It made the rest of her time trying to recover from the cancer so much more special. Thanks, Matt, and so many athletes and others who bring cheer to people on the mend.

But how do athletes learn how to give back and help in the community? Athletes for Hope (AFH) is an organization that educates and connects professional, Olympic, Paralympic, and college athletes to the charities and causes they care about. COO Jason Belinkie told me the following story. "Three years ago, the parents of a teenager in the Chicago area with terminal cancer came to them. Ty loves nothing more than the NFL and the NFL draft. Stuck in the hospital with a rare cancer, nothing they could do would bring him relief—except for thinking about the draft. A week before the draft, AFH heard from this family. Was there anything we could do for Ty regarding the draft? One hundred ten Senior Bowl athletes just signed up with us. We reached out to all of them (110), told them about Ty, and hoped for a couple of responses with some well wishes. Instead, within thirty-six hours, eighty-five athletes filmed videos for him. Remarkable, incredible, and so moving. Ten to fifteen of them even wanted his parents' phone number to call Ty and stay in touch. This helps keep the faith in humanity. But there's more. A scout from his hometown team, the Chicago Bears, heard about this and wanted to do something, too—just two days before the draft. They needed his address and phone number. They sent him a signed ball. But the coaching staff decided that wasn't enough. Coach Nagy himself called Ty the morning of the draft. Not feeling good, Ty couldn't talk to him, but the coach left him an upbeat voicemail. All the Bears filmed messages for him. The moment that he got to see these videos was the greatest moment of his life. Even in pain, it brought him such great joy. Sadly, he passed away a couple of days after the draft after having the happiest time of his life. This tremendous outreach made his life and left lasting memories for his family."

HAVE A POSITIVE ATTITUDE

What about living longer and better by thinking positively? A Yale University study found that in a group of 4,765 people with an average age of seventy-two, those who carried a gene variant linked to dementia but also had positive attitudes about aging were fifty percent less likely to develop the disorder than people who carried the gene but faced aging with more pessimism or fear. There may be something to be said for aging less timidly and looking at the sunny side of life. It's not to say that everything is always positive. Sadly, we know better—life has its ups and downs. But if we look at the glass half full rather than half empty, we have more to enjoy.

Earlier I shared the story of Ralph, whose spine is fractured and has no feeling from the chest down. But he's alive, and he wants to do things—to play clarinet, teach students, and conduct his band, elevating his wheelchair to do so—now that's a sight to see! These have all been accomplished, even performing in a benefit concert for him that clarinetists throughout Chicago put on to raise needed funds for his healthcare needs. Ralph had a choice—he could choose to live his life in anger and depression or he could say, "To heck with it, I've got a good mind and ideas, and I'm going to keep using my talent and knowledge the best way I can." Ralph chose to go with new goals, desires, and dreams to achieve. When you would think that being alive is enough after such a horrific accident, he wants to make his life worthwhile by playing and teaching beautiful music and making someone's day better.

SHARE LIFE WITH A FRIEND

Maybe you want to enjoy the opposite of where you live, either the quiet of the country or the excitement of the city. Whichever you choose, do it with a friend. A 2017 study in the *Journal of Personal Relationships* found that it can be friends, not family, who matter most. The study looked at 270,000 people in nearly one hundred countries and found that while both family and friends are associated with happiness and better health, as people aged, the health link remained only for people with strong friendships. "[While] in a lot of ways, relationships with friends had a similar effect as those with family, in others, they surpassed them," says William Chopik, assistant professor of psychology at Michigan State University. Be sure to have a good meal, take a nature walk, or enjoy a show or concert with a friend on a regular basis.

Morag Barrett has written and spoken quite a bit about the importance of connections and having a best friend at work. We spend so much time working, and if life is better with a friend, that includes working with one. I've been blessed to make friends wherever I've worked. One of the ones that comes to mind was Barry when I first came to work at Notre Dame. Barry and I just connected, and often we would take a brisk afternoon walk when weather and time permitted. It enabled us to commiserate, for me to learn from his experience having worked at the school much longer than I had, and to get some fresh air and exercise. Although our careers only overlapped for about a year before he retired, we still stay in touch, and I fondly look back at our walks as some of my best times there.

Surprise notes can be fun and unexpected, which makes them perfect. I've left notes for my wife on her mirror, pillow, in her lunch bag, and on her steering wheel. From the simple "have a great day" or "I love you" to little poems, it's the unexpected surprise that I think she appreciates most. It lets her know that I'm thinking of her. I've also put cards in her suitcase if she's travelling so that when she unpacks her suitcase, she has a nice surprise waiting for her. Make fun, surprises, and special celebrations a part of your life. Make someone's day by providing and sharing walks, stories, and special moments.

PUTTING INTO PRACTICE

Celebrations are a great way to make someone's day and, done well, become meaningful and lasting memories. Have fun, use humor, and do the unexpected. It's the surprises in life and breaks from the routine that warm our hearts, enrich our lives, and make someone's day.

Do you have a favorite birthday or moment? What made it special? How can you help your spouse, children, parents, or friends have a great celebration? Identify someone you want to do this for and make plans to make it happen.

Chapter two talked about the four-step Make Someone's Day VIP Model, but we've left step four, the R&R, for now. Chapter fourteen describes how to track and measure your effectiveness at making someone's day. Doing so will lead to a greater likelihood of making someone's day becoming a new and regular habit for you.

CHAPTER 14

· ·

TRACKING THE IMPACT AND ADVANCING YOUR PRACTICE

"If you can't measure it, you can't improve it." —Peter Drucker

THROUGHOUT THIS BOOK, YOU'VE seen how easy and effortless it is to make someone's day and the impact it has on both you and others. But how do you build your skills and grow in your practice of making someone's day? R&R—reflect and review through tracking. Here's why.

The first reason to track it is to learn what situations work best for you. The second is to improve your ability to use each element of the VIP Model. Third is to turn it into a regular habit where it becomes second nature to you. Marshall Goldsmith says that if it's important enough to you, tracking it will help make it stick. If it matters, it should be measured. Fourth, as Fred Astaire says, ". . . it takes time to create something memorable." And as a leader at work or in life, we want our actions to be memorable. Tracking and measuring your growth can be done simply enough on your own or with the help of other assessments.

For example, Human Synergistics, Inc. offers many types of lifestyle, leader, and organizational assessments based on their circumplex model. The circumplex model has twelve behavioral styles categorized in three different areas: Constructive, Aggressive/Defensive, and Passive/Defensive. Here's what that means from the founder of the company, Dr. Robert Cooke.

"Constructive styles encourage the attainment of organizational goals through people development; promote teamwork and synergy; and enhance individual, group, and organizational adaptability and effectiveness.

"Aggressive/Defensive styles lead people to focus on their own needs at the expense of those of their group and organization and lead to stress, turnover, and inconsistent performance.

"Passive/Defensive styles lead people to subordinate themselves to the organization, stifle creativity and initiative, and allow the organization to stagnate."

By taking an assessment, you can discover where your strengths are and what areas you want to develop further. And what's great about these types of assessments is you can change your rating. For those wanting to grow your constructive tendencies especially around achievement, Make Someone's Day is a great way to do this and track your progress when you retake the assessment at a later time.

Tracking can also be done simply on a spreadsheet, tally sheet, or reaction form. By tracking and recording what you experienced and how you felt, you can simply see how it impacted you and learn how to get better at making someone's day. Here's a simple tracking spreadsheet you can use that can help you track all the phases of the VIP process and any boomerang effect. Feel free to use words and phrases and, if you like, a numerical rating for the "How" questions such as 1-5.

Date/Time	What had I Viewed or observed? What did I Identify?	What did I do and for whom? (Plan and Act)	How did they react?	How did I feel afterward?

A tally sheet is easy because you can just answer with a simple yes/no. Feel free to add comments in the box.

Date/Situation	Did I make someone's day today? (Y/N)	Did I experience a boomerang effect? (Y/N)

Here's another way to track focused specifically on reactions, yours and the other person's. It can be as easy as ranking or writing answers to four simple questions each time you've made someone's day. You can use both short answers and a 1-5 (Likert) scale with 1 being low and 5 being high.

Date	How did I feel when I made someone's day?	Did I get a comment or reaction? How did that feel?	What other impact did it have on me/my day? How long did that last?	Anything I'd do differently in a similar situation? Lessons learned

Habits can take a number of months to take hold with regular practice, so don't give up! In the meantime, notice how and in what ways you making someone's day helps others and how that impacts you. Tracking can motivate you to do so more regularly. Keep the spontaneity of making someone's day, though. When those moments arise, take advantage of them. These can be the best experiences we have.

Another great way to track the impact of making someone's day is to tell stories of what happened. Stories of how others responded to you making their day. Stories of their reactions. Stories of the effort (or minimal effort) you put in to make this happen. Where else are you told that you can do as little as possible and succeed?! Share your stories and learn from others on our website howardhprager.com or on our Facebook page, facebook.com/howardhprager.

Keeping track through spreadsheets and stories is a great way to keep focused on the path to Make Someone's Day a successful habit for you.

SOME FINAL TIPS FOR IMPLEMENTING MAKE SOMEONE'S DAY

Focus on the other person, not you. That's what it's all about. When I tell my Make Someone's Day stories, it's about the reaction of others that's the point of the story. Frequently I'm amazed that they reacted in that way. (I made your day from wearing a t-shirt? From signing a petition?) In fact, sometimes the less prepared and more spontaneous I can be, the better things turn out. Share how you felt when you made someone's day. Did you experience the boomerang effect?

Tell others! How have others made your day—what did they do, and how did it impact you? Let people know they made your day. And hope they experience the boomerang effect as a result of you telling them. And remember from early on in the book, it can be the smallest of things that make your day. For example, my friend Wendy hadn't been able to respond to my emails because she was moving and sent me a positive and complimentary text the morning of our team meeting that absolutely made my day. I texted back and told her she made my day. Even through texting we can still make someone's day! And here's the key—if I hadn't told her (via text and later a phone call), she wouldn't know how it was received and may not do it again. Think how my sister felt when I told her how much I appreciated her taking our mom to musicals. Don't take it for granted; let people know how they impacted you and made your day. Too often we may think about it but don't say or do anything about it. Making someone's day is about taking that next step and doing it, saying it, and having it become a way of life.

We need to live a life with no regrets, not holding back on saying or doing things that can help make someone's day. It's too easy to do the opposite—to criticize, complain, and kvetch about the things you don't agree with or like. As I said in chapter four, it's so easy to complain that we can hardwire our brain to be a complainer or wire it to be positive and make someone's day. I know which I'm choosing. It takes a little more effort to make someone's day rather than forming the easy pathway of complaining about a situation. Reverse that now. Make the positive message at least as easy for you as the complaint, and do so frequently enough so those negative neuron pathways do not form. Keep looking for a way to have an impact on someone that makes their day. And think about your reaction when others say that you made their day.

SIX STEPS FOR INCORPORATING MAKE SOMEONE'S DAY IN YOUR LIFE

Now that you've learned the many ways to track and measure how to make someone's day, what's your next step? Here are the six steps to make Make Someone's Day part of your life.

1) **First, start easily to master making someone's day.** Start at home by complimenting your spouse, your children, or your parents. Be specific on what you're complimenting them about so they know. See their reaction. We don't do this enough in life.

2) **Use simple small talk or comment to someone while you are in line, in a waiting room, or reading someone's social media post.** They may just need that smile or comment to make their day.

I like to give my "tie of the day" award to men wearing the iconic neckwear. It's a bit more of a challenge now since so many men don't wear ties on a regular basis, so there are fewer "contestants." I just say to someone who's tie I like, "You've got the tie of the day—best I've seen." You should see the positive reaction and smile I always get. The more you do it, the more your "tie of the day" or whatever you choose will become a habit for you to do.

3) **Third, magnify your actions.** I've said to people after a presentation or performers after a concert or show, "Great job, you made my day!" When possible, I try to even be more specific so they know exactly what they said or did. "That song or story was fantastic and made my day." I even called into my favorite radio station to tell them the song they played was perfect for me.

Say something to people on the frontlines as often as you can. Let them know if they helped you or if their knowledge made your day. They don't hear it enough. Your words can have an impact on others' lives by saying something to make a flight attendant's day, train conductor's day, bus driver's day, restaurant worker's day, receptionist's day, or cashier's day. When you make their day, think about how many peoples' lives they will be touching and how they might continue to act if they are feeling more appreciated. This is the multiplier effect because by making someone's day for people who interact with the public throughout the day, they in turn can make many others' day all day long by virtue of their attitude and effort.

4) **Fourth, use this at work.** If you're a "named" leader (i.e. manage or supervise others directly), think about how you can make your direct reports' day, your bosses' day, your colleagues' day, and your service workers' day (custodian, security guard, etc.). There's probably another whole book here just on Making Someone's Day as a Leader at Work. We want the people we work with to be at their best and most productive and inspired. As a leader, this should be something you find and use frequently in your "toolkit"—ways to motivate and inspire others. Ken Blanchard says to always "catch others doing something right." Marshall Goldsmith says to "look to the future, not the past." By making someone's day, you're doing just that—helping them in a way that reinforces that they are doing the right thing, that they can look forward and continue to be their best.

5) **Fifth, use this throughout your network.** Make it a regular habit and be known in your circles as someone who inspires others. They'll benefit, and so will you. What a great reputation to have! People will

clamor to be in your network if they know you desire to make their day.

6) **Sixth, take the mystery out of it.** Let people know what you are doing and what you care about. Be conscious and conscientious about it. Don't keep it a secret because the more people that are tuned in and aware of what makes someone's day, the more they may start doing it, too, and the more people who will benefit from it. Let Make Someone's Day become something many people become a part of, and start getting the benefits of doing so yourself!

START NOW

Just start doing it sounds too simple, yet that's all it takes. Ask yourself what feels right and is easiest for you. It's not something to struggle with. Remember the four simple steps of the VIP – R+R Model.

Step 1: View/Observe the world around you, in person or online.
Step 2: Identify and determine what may be needed from what you observe.
Step 3: Plan and act, be spontaneous, or for something more involved, plan and implement it.
Step 4: Reflect and Review how you feel afterward.

CONCLUSION

Harry Kreamer, Jr., clinical professor of leadership at the Northwestern University Kellogg School and former chair and CEO of Baxter International, wrote a book called *Your 168: Finding Purpose and Satisfaction in a Values-based Life.* What is 168? The number of hours we have in a week. What is a values-based life? As Kreamer says, "Put simply, it's expressing your values in the way you want to live." Make Someone's Day is a value, and you can choose if you want to do it and include it as a part of your 168. Doing so will not take up much of your time. But the rewards you get are priceless.

I hope you'll find that with just a little effort, you can make someone's day every day and, in doing so, reap the rich intrinsic "high" from the boomerang effect that will carry you through the next hour, day, or even longer.

My desire is that Make Someone's Day becomes a movement and takes on a life of its own as many people realize that it's just as easy to make someone's day as not to. Acknowledge others and be more aware when they have made your day so they feel the boomerang effect and then continue to do this for others.

You've made my day by reading this book. Go out and make someone else's day. Get started. Don't wait. Don't doubt yourself. Once you do it and see the impact, you'll wonder why you didn't try to make someone's day sooner and even identify situations where you have already been making someone's day. It can be that easy.

Helen Keller said, "When one door of happiness closes, another opens, but often we look so long at the closed door that we do not see the one that has been opened for us." Keep your eyes and ears alert for the open doors to make someone's day today!

Continue your journey to Make Someone's Day a part of your life!

ACKNOWLEDGMENTS

· ·

THERE ARE PROBABLY A million people I'd like to thank who have helped me get here. The first and foremost is my wife Laurie, who put up with me during the long process of writing and the never-ending process of editing and reviewing my work. Second goes to my sister Merril and brother-in-law John, who were so supportive and let me bounce ideas off them every step of the way, and my daughter Hillary, who joined me on many outings to make someone's day, created my website, and provided technical guidance. Third, everyone I interviewed who shared your stories with me. Thank you for brightening our world with your touching and beautiful examples. And to all the people who helped make my day throughout my life and who have allowed me to make theirs, I thank you and keep you all close in my memory.

My book project manager and advisor Stacey Crew provided great insight and guidance through the whole process. Maddie Miles started as my intern and became my social media expert who has helped with many aspects, including my monthly newsletter updates. Without each of you, this wouldn't have happened as well. Thanks as well to the publisher John Koehler and the team at Koehler Books, much gratitude to you.

There are some special groups of people who provided insight and advice, many of whom stem from my affiliation with Marshall Goldsmith and the 100 Coaches. Marshall, thank you for the beautiful foreword, advice, and support. My Life Plan Review team Morag Barrett, Cynthia Burnham, John Baldoni, Deepa Prahalad, Lacey McLaughlin, and Evelyn Rodstein—you inspire me each week. My book mastermind group of Doug Winnie, CB Bowman, and Nankhonde-Kasonde Van den Broek— we made it! My two Coaches Connect groups, Team Alpha with Rob, David, Lucrecia, Beth, Curtis, Andrew, and Morag. And Team Echo with Scott, Caroline, Saskia, Charlene, Michel, Mahesh, and Cynthia again. And to my daily questions partner, Johannes Coloma-Flecker, your support, insights, and friendship are always appreciated.

Because of COVID-19, some different groups became sounding boards, including Jim and Harriette's Wednesday dance group with Mary, Jim, Harriette, Dori, Alan, and Karen. We didn't just dance on Zoom, you provided helpful input and support during our chats. My Association of Talent Development best buds who have all been chapter leaders as we shared our life's work together. Each of you live Make Someone's Day and inspire me as a leader. Rick Hicks, Rebecca Boyle, Joe Willmore, Lea Toppino, Sardek Love, Maureen Orey, Sharon Wingron, Kathy Shurte, Kimo Kippen, Rita Bailey, Jack and Patti Phillips, Ken Phillips, Deborah Covin Wilson, and many others. My high school buddies and lifelong friends, thanks for always asking about my progress as we have all been there for each other, and all the great musician friends I've played with and who inspire me with your talent. My best men, Ron, Ralph, and Ted, each of you is always just a call away. To Rabbi Debra Newman Kamin, thanks for your steadfast support and thanks to congregants at Am Yisrael and Temple Chai who became early enthusiasts. And to my fellow Scouters who all care about helping youth develop into productive and valued contributors to society, we need more people like you. Because there's a new generation coming that need to live Make Someone's Day!

REFERENCES

....

INTRODUCTION

Grant, Adam M. *Give and Take: the Hidden Social Dynamics of Success.* New York, NY: Viking, 2013.

CHAPTER 3

Ritvo, Eva. "The Neuroscience of Giving." Psychology Today. Sussex Publishers, April 14, 2014. https://www.psychologytoday.com/us/blog/the-beauty-prescription/201404/the-neuroscience-giving.

Duermyer, Randy. "How LinkedIn Works and Helps Your Business or Career." The Balance Small Business, December 1, 2020. https://www.thebalancesmb.com/introduction-to-linkedin-1794572.

Cutler, Jo, and Robin Banerjee. "Five Reasons Why Being Kind Makes You Feel Good – According to Science." The Conversation, February 26, 2018. http://theconversation.com/five-reasons-why-being-kind-makes-you-feel-good-according-to-science-92459.

Davis, Jeanie Lerche. "The Science of Good Deeds." WebMD. WebMD, 2005. https://www.webmd.com/balance/features/science-good-deeds#1.

CHAPTER 4

Stevenson, Sarah. "There's Magic in Your Smile." Psychology Today. Sussex Publishers, June 25, 2012. https://www.psychologytoday.com/us/blog/cutting-edge-leadership/201206/there-s-magic-in-your-smile.

Marano, Hara Estroff. "The Art of the Compliment." Psychology Today. Sussex Publishers, March 1, 2004. https://www.psychologytoday. com/us/articles/200403/the-art-the-compliment.

CHAPTER 5

Epstein, Angela. "The Proof That Visiting People in Hospital Really Does Them Good." Daily Mail Online. Associated Newspapers, October 16, 2006. https://www.dailymail.co.uk/health/article-410783/The-proof-visiting-people-hospital-really-does-good.html.

Post, Jennifer. "Why a Positive Attitude in the Workplace Matters." Business News Daily, October 1, 2019. https://www.businessnewsdaily. com/6912-develop-positive-mindset.html.

Kochevar, Jean Ann. "Value of Volunteering: Acts Small and Large Priceless." The Business Times, March 7, 2012. http://thebusinesstimes.com/ value-of-volunteering-acts-small-and-large-priceless/.

Pollak, Lindsey. *Recalculating: Navigate Your Career through the Changing World of Work.* New York, NY: Harper Business, an imprint of HarperCollinsPublishers, 2021.

Schein, Peter A., and Edgar H. Schein. *Humble Inquiry: The Gentle Art of Asking Instead of Telling, Second Edition, Revised and Expanded.* Oakland, CA: Berrett-Koehler, 2021.

CHAPTER 6

William, David K. "15 Things Introverts Don't Do At Work That Makes Them Excel." Lifehack. Lifehack, August 14, 2017. https://www. lifehack.org/articles/work/15-things-introverts-dont-work-that-makes-them-excel.html.

Park, Christina. "Eight Ways For Introverts To Shine At Work." Forbes. Forbes Magazine, October 15, 2014. https://www.forbes.com/sites/christinapark/2014/10/03/eight-ways-for-introverts-to-shine-at-work/#9cf3e4e43fd1.

Lawrence, Ali. "20 Websites That Can Help You Make a Difference." Millennial Magazine. Ali Lawrence, October 20, 2015. https://millennialmagazine.com/2015/10/20/20-websites-that-can-help-you-make-a-difference/.

Seiter, Courtney. "The Secret Psychology of Facebook: Why We Like, Share, Comment and Keep Coming Back." Buffer Resources. Buffer Resources, June 30, 2020. https://blog.bufferapp.com/psychology-of-facebook.

D'Costa, Krystal. "What Does It Mean to Be an Introvert Online?" Scientific American Blog Network. Scientific American, March 27, 2014. https://blogs.scientificamerican.com/anthropology-in-practice/what-does-it-mean-to-be-an-introvert-online/.

Stevenson, Sarah. "There's Magic in Your Smile." Psychology Today. Sussex Publishers, June 25, 2012. https://www.psychologytoday.com/us/blog/cutting-edge-leadership/201206/there-s-magic-in-your-smile.

Goldstein, Elisha. *The Now Effect: How a Mindful Moment Can Change the Rest of Your Life*. London: Atria Books, 2013.

McCarthy, Jeremy. "The Power of a Smile and a Nod." The Psychology of Wellbeing, November 23, 2012. http://psychologyofwellbeing.com/201211/the-power-of-a-smile-and-a-nod.html.

Digital, Start. "The Psychology of Being 'Liked' on Social Media." Medium. The Startup, January 27, 2018. https://medium.com/swlh/likes-on-social-media-87bfff679602.

Spector, Nicole. "Smiling Can Trick Your Brain into Happiness - and Boost Your Health." NBCNews.com. NBCUniversal News Group, January 10, 2018. https://www.nbcnews.com/better/health/smiling-can-trick-your-brain-happiness-boost-your-health-ncna822591.

"Social Media 'Likes' Impact Teens' Brains and Behavior." Association for Psychological Science - APS, May 31, 2016. https://www.psychologicalscience.org/news/releases/social-media-likes-impact-teens-brains-and-behavior.html.

Murthy, Vivek. "Together by Dr. Vivek Murthy." drvivekmurthy. Accessed July 18, 2021. https://www.vivekmurthy.com/together-book.

CHAPTER 7

Flavin, Brianna. "6 Surprising Health Benefits of Donating Blood." 6 Surprising Health Benefits of Donating Blood | Rasmussen University, February 1, 2018. http://www.rasmussen.edu/degrees/health-sciences/blog/surprising-health-benefits-of-donating-blood/.

"Maimonides' Eight Levels of Charity." Chabad.org, n.d. https://www.chabad.org/library/article_cdo/aid/45907/jewish/Eight-Levels-of-Charity.htm.

Leibrock, Amy. "How to Start a Shared Garden." Sustainable America. Accessed July 18, 2021. http://www.sustainableamerica.org/blog/how-to-start-a-garden-share/.

CHAPTER 8

Llopis, Glenn. "8 Qualities That Make Leaders Memorable." Forbes. Forbes Magazine, January 13, 2014. https://www.forbes.com/sites/glennllopis/2014/01/13/8-qualities-that-make-leaders-extraordinarily-memorable/?sh=6b8806437565.

Wright, Brian K. "How to Build a Culture of Appreciation in Your Organization." Accessed January 2020. https://drbobnelson.com/wp-content/uploads/2020/01/dr.bob-success-mag.11.27.19-1-1.pdf.

"My Best Boss - Stories of the Greatest Bosses of All Time." Quickbase, June 5, 2014. https://www.quickbase.com/blog/my-best-boss-stories-of-the-greatest-bosses-of-all-time.

Mautz, Scott. "Employees Crave More Appreciation From Their Bosses, Research Shows. Here's How to Better Appreciate Your Team." Inc. com. Inc., September 28, 2019. https://www.inc.com/scott-mautz/employees-crave-more-appreciation-from-their-bosses-research-shows-heres-how-to-better-appreciate-your-team.html.

"The Future of Work Is Human." Workhuman. The Workhuman Analytics & Research Institute, 2019. https://www.workhuman.com/press-releases/White_Paper_The_Future_of_Work_is_Human.pdf.

Blanchard, Kenneth H., and Spencer Johnson. *The New One Minute Manager*. New York, NY: William Morrow, an imprint of HarperCollinsPublishers, 2015.

Joly, Hubert, and Caroline Lambert. *The Heart of Business: Leadership Principles for the next Era of Capitalism*. Boston, MA: Harvard Business Review Press, 2021.

CHAPTER 9

Hartman, Steve. "How to Participate in Steve Hartman's 'Taps Across America.'" CBS News. CBS Interactive, May 26, 2020. https://www.cbsnews.com/news/how-to-participate-in-steve-hartmans-taps-across-america/.

Luc, Karie Angell. "Highwood Nonprofit Holds Grocery Giveaway as the COVID-19 Pandemic Rages On." chicagotribune.com. Chicago Tribune, July 20, 2020. https://www.chicagotribune.com/suburbs/highland-park/ct-hpn-highwood-food-giveaway-covid-tl-0723-20200720-vs2wnzojuneznba424ibvx4eiq-story.html.

Cunningham, Katie. "'People Need to Be Supportive': Communities Gather Online in the Coronavirus Crisis." The Guardian. Guardian News and Media, March 16, 2020. https://www.theguardian.com/lifeandstyle/2020/mar/17/people-need-to-be-supportive-finding-community-online-in-the-coronavirus-crisis.

Doheny, Kathleen. "COVID-19 & Kindness: 'Caremongering' Is Trending." WebMD. WebMD, March 20, 2020. https://www.webmd.com/lung/news/20200320/covid-19-kindness-caremongering-is-trending?ecd=wnl_spr_032120&ctr=wnl-spr-032120_nsl-Bodymodule_Position3&mb=I0nXikyd%40qRKqzqkRl%2FOE5AyWFWqf9PLb8xlMIOWR7U%3D.

NBC Chicago. "Students Launch Fee-Free Shopping Service to Help Senior Citizens Get Food, Prescriptions." NBC Chicago. NBC Chicago, March 22, 2020. https://www.nbcchicago.com/news/local/students-launch-fee-free-shopping-service-to-help-senior-citizens-get-food-prescriptions/2242479/.

CHAPTER 10

Porath, Christine. "An Antidote to Incivility." Harvard Business Review, June 9, 2016. https://hbr.org/2016/04/an-antidote-to-incivility.

Porath, Christine Lynne. *Mastering Civility: a Manifesto for the Workplace*. New York, NY: Grand Central Publishing, 2016.

Porath, Christine L., and Amir Erez. "Does Rudeness Really Matter? The Effects of Rudeness on Task Performance and Helpfulness." *The Academy of Management Journal* 50, no. 5 (2007): 1181-197. Accessed July 18, 2021. doi:10.2307/20159919.

Porath, Christine. "How Rudeness Takes Its Toll." How rudeness takes its toll | The Psychologist, July 2011. https://thepsychologist.bps.org.uk/volume-24/edition-7/how-rudeness-takes-its-toll#.

Sack, David. "The 5 Traits of Extraordinary Ordinary People." Psychology Today. Sussex Publishers, March 31, 2015. https://www.psychologytoday.com/us/blog/where-science-meets-the-steps/201503/the-5-traits-extraordinary-ordinary-people.

"Amir Erez at UF Warrington College of Business." Directory. Accessed July 18, 2021. http://warrington.ufl.edu/contact/profile.asp?WEBID=2057.

CHAPTER 11

Su, Elizabeth. "What Gratitude Does to Your Brain." Thrive Global, November 27, 2018. https://thriveglobal.com/stories/gratitude-brain-positive-change-thank-you/?utm_campaign=buffer&utm_content=buffer09600&utm_medium=Arianna&utm_source=LinkedIn.

"Family Today: A Study of US Families." AARP, September 2012. https://www.aarp.org/content/dam/aarp/research/surveys_statistics/general/2012/Family-Today-A-Study-of-US-Families-AARP.pdf.

Sloan, Carrie. "Can You Change Unhealthy Family Patterns?" WebMD. WebMD. Accessed July 18, 2021. https://www.webmd.com/balance/features/can-you-change-unhealthy-family-patterns.

CHAPTER 12

Pinter, Jacob. "An NYC Scout Troop Provides Homeless Girls A Place Of Their Own." NPR. NPR, July 26, 2017. https://www.npr.org/2017/07/26/538551816/a-nyc-scout-troop-provides-homeless-girls-a-place-of-their-own#:~:text=Live%20Sessions-,An%20NYC%20Scout%20Troop%20Provides%20Homeless%20Girls%20A%20Place%20Of,for%20girls%20who%20are%20homeless.

CHAPTER 13

Kluger, Jeffrey, and Alexandra Sifferlin. "The Secrets to Living a Longer and Better Life." Time. Time, February 15, 2018. http://time.com/5159852/the-surprising-secrets-to-living-longer-and-better/.

LoVerme Akhtar, Vanessa. "What CEOs Can Learn From Colbert And Kimmel." Forbes. Forbes Magazine, April 30, 2018. https://www.forbes.com/sites/johnkotter/2018/04/30/what-ceos-can-learn-from-colbert-and-kimmel/#3c65d2d233a4.

Smith, Jacquelyn. "10 Reasons Why Humor Is A Key To Success At Work." Forbes. Forbes Magazine, June 20, 2014. https://www.forbes.com/sites/jacquelynsmith/2013/05/03/10-reasons-why-humor-is-a-key-to-success-at-work/#2d12d9a65c90.

Gruber, Bryce. "8 Outrageous Marriage Proposals You Have to Read to Believe." Reader's Digest. Reader's Digest, July 2, 2021. https://www.rd.com/true-stories/love/outrageous-marriage-proposals/.

CHAPTER 14

Jansen, Kraemer Harry M. *Your 168: Finding Purpose and Satisfaction in a Values-Based Life.* Hoboken, NJ: John Wiley & Sons, Inc., 2020.

CPSIA information can be obtained
at www.ICGtesting.com
Printed in the USA
LVHW090844011021
699214LV00001B/68